ON WRITING
THE SHORT STORY

OTHER BOOKS
BY HALLIE BURNETT

ON WRITING THE SHORT STORY

Hallie Burnett

1817

HARPER & ROW, PUBLISHERS, New York

Cambridge, Philadelphia, San Francisco, London
Mexico City, São Paulo, Sydney

Grateful acknowledgment is made for permission to reprint: "Indian Summer" by Erskine Caldwell, reprinted by permission of McIntosh and Otis, Inc. "Address Unknown" by Kressmann Taylor first appeared in the September/October 1938 issue of *STORY* Magazine; copyright 1938 by Kressmann Taylor, reprinted by permission of William Morris Agency, Inc. on behalf of the author. "The Most Important Thing" by Tennessee Williams from *One Arm & Other Stories* by Tennessee Williams, copyright 1945 by Tennessee Williams, is reprinted by permission of New Directions Publishing Corporation and Elaine Green Ltd (London, England). "My Side of the Matter" by Truman Capote from *A Tree of Night and Other Stories* by Truman Capote, copyright 1945 by Truman Capote, is reprinted by permission of Random House, Inc.

FIRST EDITION

Designer: Jane Weinberger

Library of Congress Cataloging in Publication Data

Burnett, Hallie Southgate,
  On writing the short story.

  Includes index.
  1. Short story. 2. Fiction—Authorship. I. Title.
PN3373.B78 1983   808.3   82-48111
ISBN 0-06-015094-7

83 84 85 86 87 10 9 8 7 6 5 4 3 2 1

For
John Southgate Burnett
and
Louisa Zamparutti
with love

CONTENTS

A Minor Introduction
by the Author

I AM an addict of short stories, those I read and those I write. Some critics may object to this linking of great masterworks with the twenty or forty short stories I have had published, but you, the writer, will understand. You know as as well as I the early delights of first discovering and then absorbing the stories of the masters— of Anton Chekhov and Stephen Crane and James Joyce, of Katherine Anne Porter and Ernest Hemingway, Somerset Maugham, Sherwood Anderson, James Thurber, and on and on and on, through our own explorations in this rich and time-honored art form.

But if you are also born with the itch to conjure up your own fantasies about the life you see around you, about the human condition and about characters as absurd, varied, unpredictable, tragic, joyous, destructive, and baffling as any already absorbed from your fiction reading, you know that one obsession may not exist without the other—that is, if you would be a writer. Above all, a writer of short and, one hopes, memorable fiction.

I have in my possession the first short story I ever wrote, at the age of seven. Untitled, it was for my grandmother, and related the adventure of a bad little girl who was cheerful, and a good little boy who worried a lot. I like to think the theme showed a certain authorial independence for that age, which perhaps sheds some light on the mind of a fiction writer: from the beginning we are inclined to turn upside down the reliability of everything we are told.

Nor is there any reason to believe everything you read in this book, although I trust the examples of other working writers will help clarify your own thinking, your working habits, and your own resolve. It has been said that creativity is nothing more than the urge to bring order out of the chaos of the universe. I accept this, but I add a little more: I would say it is also, for the writer, an excuse to examine everything, rejecting nothing other than sentimentality, redundancy, self-pity, didacticism, bad grammar, bigotry, and laziness. It is also a God-given means of avoiding boredom and stagnation to the end of one's days.

H. B.

ON WRITING
THE SHORT STORY

1

What Is a Story?
What Makes a Story Writer?

THE SHORT STORY has as many faces and as many moods as all humanity. It is the earliest and most natural of literary forms, and the most durable. It is the most democratic of all the arts; anyone may tell a story, and if it is an absorbing one someone will listen. The good story reduces drama and common human experience to their essence. Being short and to the point, it will focus on a moment, or a year, or maybe a lifetime, providing drama, wit, irony, humor, or tragedy. Whether it is written in the English language, the French, German, Spanish, Italian, or Greek or Hebrew, its narrator, by means of anecdote, gossip, wisdom, or dramatic emphasis, will in less than an hour's time arouse, amuse, enlist, or provoke listeners and readers alike.

The short story form as we know it today has roots developed from Greek mythology, Aesop's fables, Chaucerian contemporary tales, French *contes*, Italian novellas, and German *Novellen*. Then came the sketches of Washington Irving, the tales of Hawthorne, Poe, Melville, Mark Twain, de Maupassant, Chekhov, and Henry James. In our time we have had Ernest Hemingway, Sherwood Anderson, F. Scott Fitzgerald, Katherine Anne Porter, William Faulkner, John

Updike, John Cheever, Flannery O'Connor, Bernard Malamud, Eudora Welty—and there are all those talented new writers whose work vivifies and examines the realities of today.

What is a story? Erskine Caldwell defines it best as "an imaginary tale with a meaning, interesting enough to hold the reader's attention, profound enough to express human nature." It does not matter where the reader's attention has been directed, so long as it is stimulated and held. Our only concern as readers is, to paraphrase Chekhov, Did it keep you awake? Did it shock? Did it amuse? Did it send you away feeling you have had an experience more absorbing than any in your own life? Katherine Anne Porter defines the story from the perspective of the writer: the short story presents "first a theme, then a point of view; a certain knowledge of human nature and strong feeling about it; and style."

The essential ingredient, however, is the story itself. An impatient editor once wrote to Paul Gallico, author of *The Snow Goose*, a memorable tale of World War II, "I don't care what your background is if you will *just tell me a story!*"

It has been said that everyone has at least one story to tell: his own. The writer, however, must have many more than his own: those of his friends, his lovers, children, and strangers he will meet. It is through the fascinating variety of other minds and emotions and acts that the writer must probe, if he is to be a writer, for his materials. It is by the exercise and honing of his talents that this material will be transformed into professional work that will eventually attract the audience it must have. The artist only seems to exist in a vacuum; he does not write just for himself, even though he must satisfy his own standards of excellence first. The act is finally complete when the author's story has made contact with the mind of a reader.

Somerset Maugham has reminded us that nothing happens in a writer's life which he cannot use, and it could be added that no person, no friend or foe or even stranger passing through a writer's consciousness is unworthy of his notice and reflection. Thus, the starting point in the search for his material will be the writer's own experiences and encounters. Yet it will be his talent alone that makes fictional art from the amusing, tragic, boring, or apocalyptic moments felt or observed in the lives around him.

Sherwood Anderson's early tales in *Winesburg, Ohio* revealed to countless short story writers how to use the seemingly haphazard contacts brought before us in daily life—the experiences taking place before our eyes and those glimpsed peripherally and unexpectedly. Often, in Anderson's stories, the experience was simply that of a boy growing up in a small midwestern town, trying to understand himself (one story is entitled "I Want to Know Why") and his elders' often disturbing behavior in the unforeseeable accidents of living and loving, which the writer first observed and then recorded in his fiction. The writer is one who starts early and very privately to make such observations and to store these, often unconsciously, in his memory bank for future use.

Effective short stories come also from the sometimes daring or exaggerated uses of the imagination. Anthony Trollope related how, as a lonely boy, he was thrown back much upon himself, so that "play of some kind was necessary." He writes in *An Autobiography*, "I was always going about with some castle in the air firmly built within my mind. . . . For weeks, for months, from year to year," he would carry on the same task of continuing this imaginary fable. "I learned in this way to maintain interest in a fictitious story, to dwell on a work created [solely] by my own imagination. . . . I doubt, had it not been for my practice, I should ever have written a book."

This, for writers of fiction, brings us to an essential which cannot be stressed often enough: the strength of our belief in the story we relate. One must deeply and profoundly believe in the direction of one's imagination and, while at work, in the story waiting to be told. A writer must practice, to a profound degree, the "suspension of disbelief." He must not only care about what he is writing, he must believe without question that he is re-creating truth, that the truth of his story is what it must be, and let no one be in any doubt about that. And, if one writes as believingly as possible, the story will then ring true for the reader.

This vital concern for conviction is a kind of conspiracy. It begins best with knowledge of the self, which the writer then extends to others. Generally speaking, of course, this process is inevitable in our evaluation of all that goes on around us. But as we observe our friends, lovers, and enemies, as writers we must have for them the feelings of sympathy, empathy, understanding, guilt, or regret that inevitably we give ourselves. It is the only way, then, that a reader eventually can feel closeness with characters so far outside of his actual experience. It is thus that writers like Franz Kafka, Tennessee Williams, and Anton Chekhov seem to reveal to all of us the secrets of the human race, the deepest truths about ourselves.

And if this involvement is lacking in your own work, your story will leave a reader cold and probably disbelieving of all you have to say, because it has come from you with no real emotional persuasion. Any reasonably perceptive reader will spot this coldness, this lack of true commitment on the writer's part, just as a musically perceptive concert audience will wince at a false or misplaced note.

The painter Robert Henri's advice to the novice is also valid for the writer: "For the artist to be interesting to us he must have been interesting to himself. He must have been capable of intense feeling, and capable of profound contemplation. . . . Whether he wills it or not, each brush stroke is an exact record of such as he was at the exact moment the stroke was made."

Henri's profound observation that the artist and his work are inseparable—that the artist "is," in some sense, also his creation—was phrased differently by the great actress Ethel Barrymore in her advice to young actors. "Learn day by day, year by year, to broaden your horizon. The more things you love, the more things you are interested in, the more pleasures you enjoy, the more you are indignant about . . . the more perceptively you will identify with your creation, the better prepared you are to be an actor." Or a painter. Or a fiction writer. For both the actor and the writer—for any artist—the human truths we are creating or re-creating, the story we are telling or the drama we are acting, must be intensely real in that private world we are each privileged to call our own.

The psychologist Carl Jung has put it another way. "Fascination," he says "is the key. Once you find yourself totally fascinated by anything, you will, if you are in control of the necessary disciplines, use it to enlarge your talent." And this fascination need not be focused on the ordinary or the easily understood so much as on the *felt* experience. Often enough it is the alien, the strange, that will catch our attention and from which we work to enlarge our understanding.

Some men write compellingly about women. D. H. Lawrence, who loved women, could reveal hidden thoughts and reactions in a woman character which many female writers find beyond their capacity to reveal except in autobiography. Some women have written with remarkable understanding about men. Many of both sexes have failed in writing about what to them is the second sex.

The world of childhood can be an alien place to those who have left it behind, but some masters of the short story have managed to remember and re-create it. D. H. Lawrence, in "The Rocking-Horse Winner," tells us of the unexpected gift a child discovers for predicting winning racehorses, but so compulsive becomes his youthful passion that he is destroyed by its intensity. Katherine Mansfield, in re-creating her childhood in New Zealand, has given us the imaginary world of children with unsurpassed insight into their hearts and minds.

J. D. Salinger crossed gender and age boundaries so well that one critic has said: "I don't like Salinger. He tells us too much—more than we *want* to know." With his unique talent he gave us characters not easily identifiable in an adult world, and yet compellingly believable. One little-known story of Salinger's "The Long Debut of Lois Taggett," shows a 180-degree turn outward from Sherwood Anderson's early fiction (although both writers obviously lived intensely with the youths they once had been). This story concerns a girl, Lois Taggett, who makes her debut in New York society, marries without love or passion, has a baby and loses it, and in the end rises above tragedy and disappointment to mature as a compassionate human being capable of love and faith. Lois, initially a frivolous and self-absorbed character who could be passed over easily because of the inconsequential quality of her existence, yet suggests to Salinger the same troubled human experience that Anderson probed in the darker aspects of life and death seen and felt around him in another part of the world.

The more unforgettable tales of any generation, the short stories or stories in the expanded form of the novellas, seem always to have developed naturally from such intense and fascinated observation and, often, personal identification. Scott Fitzgerald's "The Diamond As Big As the Ritz," Hemingway's "The Snows of Kilimanjaro," Tolstoi's "The Death of Ivan Ilyich," and Thomas Mann's *Death in Venice* each must have had its origin first in the author's sensitivity to his own reactions and feelings, then in the capacity of his imagination to take off into conjecture, recognition, and finally transformation, through skill and logic and individual genius, to develop these into enduring works of art. A memorable story is an ideal *mariage à trois*, of feeling, imagination, and certainly inspiration, which may happen only once in a lifetime—or again may frequently be possible to the writer with sufficient talent and concentration and staying power in his art.

To the outside observer, a fine short story, also like the ideal marriage, seems to have been easily achieved. To the participant, or writer, it is another matter—of love, doubt, desire, negotiation, work, and trust.

Robert Frost once said, "Every general who goes into battle wishes he had more information before he goes in. Each crisis you go into is on insufficient information." This is true of the writer at any time in his career. Preparations for the battle must be made, but precisely how to mount the attack, overcome initial resistances, and be pre-

6

pared for the outcome if one does, or does not, achieve the winning strike, is up to you, the writer. Yet a good short story *is* a battle won, and should promise more victories tomorrow.

Your first step was probably taken long before the present moment, even before words were put upon any page. Yet now, before bothering to read advice to writers published in innumerable books and magazines, or spend time and money taking university extension courses or attending writers' conferences, leaving behind perhaps a mate and a few puzzled children, one should ask oneself this question: Why do I want to write? What drives me toward trying to create a world in fictional terms, instead of becoming a bookkeeper, teacher, advertising copywriter, or atomic physicist, all careers where one would find some dependable guideposts along the way and encounter more friendly faces, keep the wolf from the door, and manage to live a sensible and regular life? In short, *why write?*

As in most human endeavors, desire and the chances for success go hand in hand. Pin a writer to the wall, ask him the preceding questions, and he may echo the words of Robert Frost: "Because I don't get the same satisfaction from doing anything else." If you can say simply that writing seems to provide a more exciting state of mind than any other; that conversations you hear interest you more than music that will command an orchestra, or equations that when solved might destroy or save a universe; that words, once you start writing, or even before, taste like caviar on the tongue, then relax, take a deep breath, and prepare to work hard at your chosen trade. You could have a good life, even if you don't hit the best-seller lists; even if your acquaintances don't see the good reviews but only the poor ones; even if your best friend (or husband or wife) wonders why you don't turn out masterpieces in an hour or so instead of in a month or a year or more. Just put a bold face on for criticizing friends and relatives, take experience as it comes, and hold on.

And then there is the search for truth.

"Almost any child is born with the hope that the universe is somehow to be explained," Elizabeth Bowen wrote. "It may be, the writer does not outlive that hope." The writer is, first and last, a believer in the strength and revelation of the written word, and his desire to explain the universe through language rarely leaves him.

"This is the only way one can ever find the truth," Jean Malaquais, the novelist, once said to Norman Mailer. "The only time I know that something is true is at the moment I discover it in the act of writing.

"I write entirely to find out what I'm thinking, what I'm looking at, what I see and what it means. What I want, and what I fear. What is going on in these pictures in my mind."

Frank O'Connor reminds us in his fine book on writing that a short story can reveal the truth "in a way that the novel [even] with its wider canvas cannot achieve."

Is the *desire* to write enough? How do I know I am a writer? is a question often asked of those of us who talk and write and lecture on the short story. What characteristics are most essential to those of us who wish to succeed?

As in any art form, the quick answer is relatively easy. You have the desire. The talent. You are willing to practice. You add to these, persistence; stubbornness in the face of rejection; the habit of self-criticism, and faith in yourself, in equal parts. And always you will remember that if a writer withholds his vital self, ignores the promptings of his own unique "daemon," as Rudyard Kipling has said, he will not succeed nor will he be read or long remembered. "When your daemon is in charge, do not try to think, consciously," wrote Kipling. "Drift, wait, and obey."

But not too long a drift. Not too patient a wait. And be quick to obey your daemon the moment he first most forcefully raises up his head.

2

The Search for a Story to Tell: Memory and Plot

"I DO NOT THINK you can write a good short story without having a good story in you," Whit Burnett used to tell his class at Columbia University. "I would rather you had something to say with no technique, than have technique with nothing to say."

"Something to say" is assuredly of first importance when we presume to demand the attentions of a reader: we owe him no less than that. We ask his attention, perhaps an hour out of his life, and even his affection. We perform on the printed page as actors: yet at the same time, without sight or sound, the final interpretation must be the reader's own. If our story—or act, if you will—has failed to interest, stimulate, or evoke some responsive emotion, he will not wish to read us again.

So our problem at the beginning is, How do we know when we have a story to tell? Can we be sure a particular episode, mood, character, or observation has weight and significance enough to justify the telling?

Unfortunately, we can never be quite sure. We may only say that having absorbed certain experiences and observations of ourselves and our fellow human beings, having identified the need to communicate all this through the form of the short story, and having realized that we care enough for language so that each word must satisfy us before we let it stand, then having recognized all these things, we are entitled to some degree of confidence.

It may sound simple, and of course it is not. For now as a serious writer one must speak with one's own voice rather than in imitation of any other that has spoken before. We must work to produce the image of our unique vision, so that the words on the page come to life as surely as a child is born in the process of human reproduction.

This does not mean that the theme—or even the plot, background, and facts—need be absolutely new. Human nature has not changed much over the centuries. But each person's experience of existence is unique and the good short story must seem to be telling us something fresh and significant. (One does not borrow another writer's clothes in creating a short story, nor attempt to wear those purchased from another.) In the circular room of E. M. Forster's *Some Aspects of the Novel*, five writers sit around a table. Each of them, given the same subject, Forster remarked, will produce a different story—his own.

Next comes the problem of deciding which, among all the characters, experiences, and ideas accumulated in the eager and retentive mind, you will use. Which story will you tell? How will you decide where your commitment and your energies should be focused?

Similarly, Anthony Trollope revealed that he never knew, when he began, where a story would end; a plot need not have been entirely clear in his mind before he started to write, he confessed. Elizabeth Bowen has spoken eloquently of the writer's "roving eye," which sees everything in a perpetual state of wonder. The writer does not necessarily search for his subject, she says. Like a child, he exists in a "state of open susceptibility," and, more often than not, the subject finds the writer. A compelling face or object, an overheard phrase, "the reverberation after a street accident or tiny subjective echo of a huge world event"—almost anything may attract the attention and seize the imagination, stimulating the narrative flow. *Fascination* again is the key element which at any given moment may be stimulus enough to start the writer on that voyage of exploration and discovery that characterizes the short story at its best. From here on, the writer's own skills and subconscious, his busyness of mind and senses, take over and creation can begin if the scene presented then jolts the memory into making connections. A mere chronicle of observed events will produce only journalism; combined with a sensitive memory, it can produce art.

But how capricious memory can be in that process of storing pictures and phrases in the mind! A particular face, disconnected scenes, words, matters which may seem utterly irrelevant to one's current interests or preoccupations can uncomfortably interrupt the process of daily life. What possible relevance can an opponent's cheating in a game long since ended have for the present moment? Why should an insult suffered years ago, and apparently forgotten, surface suddenly to consciousness? Why do I find myself pondering the possible causes of expired action by someone who personally should mean nothing to me, or studying my own reactions and those of others best forgotten? Why wonder about the lives of perfect strangers?

The answer is that nothing that passes through the writer's consciousness will go unexamined or unreflected upon. Nothing that has ever shocked, startled, hurt, pleased, or amused is simply dismissed. Of those faces you pass on the street one or two will be remembered. Consciously or unconsciously, you will have recorded a facial expression, a carriage or stride of the body, a silhouette, an impression of nerves or nervelessness—anything may be part of this brief flash of recognition. And someday all this will come back to you even though you may never have intended to have it brought back, may indeed have long since forgotten when or where the impression was made. For the writer's brain is a storehouse as well as an instrument through which life itself is renewed each day; it is from the fortunate combination of both that fiction is created.

As a writer you may feel there has been a sort of plan in all this,

11

that it was intended for a certain memory to link up with other stored memories, emotions, and unresolved conflicts. Without this special kind of awareness of all that has passed through your life, without an appreciation of its impact on the present, it is unlikely that you will ever be a writer.

It was with my first commercially published story, "Eighteenth Summer," that I learned how valuable—if capricious—memory can be. The story was based on an episode from my late adolescence some years before, which had not seemed personally important to me at the time. Yet more than ten years afterward, when I thought I had forgotten the event and the mood it engendered, another chance meeting suddenly connected with memory, and the story came full-blown, almost wrote itself, with more complexity and emotion than I could possibly have anticipated.

When I was a teenager, I spent a winter with my mother in California, where I went to Hollywood High School—a relatively pleasant, untroubled time when I made friends easily and became part of a group with no particular problems or aims in life. We danced, we swam, we kissed, and I think we talked a lot. Whether we were all still virginal I did not know and don't think it mattered very much. Naturally we were already healthily wired for sexual currents which would be turned on before long, but at that time all this seemed ahead of most of us, and we were in no hurry. Friendships, school, and even parents actually had greater importance in our lives, and we could have continued for some time longer in this untroubled state of innocence if the incident of my story had not occurred.

It was one night at a party when things changed, when into a relatively untroubled atmosphere a new element was introduced.

We had gathered at the home of a friend, with no parents present, which was only slightly unusual, and were dancing to records, when one of the boys, a familiar member of our crowd, arrived at the party with a girl who quite definitely was not. She was young enough, but obviously much older in experience and intentions; a little cheap, perhaps, but somehow fascinating to us in an oddly disturbing way. The party had not been under way very long when the two of them slipped into a downstairs bedroom and locked the door.

Very soon after, with the party mood inexplicably changed, the rest of us decided to go on to another house, and one of us called out to the couple behind those locked doors that we were leaving. There came an angry, emotional response from the boy—our friend, whom we thought we knew so well—to get out! to leave them alone!

That was it. That was the total memory and the event.

Ten years later, at another party, I met another girl whose same defiant sexuality altered the atmosphere, a situation which I could then recognize for what it was. The next day I wrote the story, "Eighteenth Summer," with quick strokes and no delay. I did, however, make significant changes in the process of turning these facts into fiction. The physical appearance of the girl at the second party became the catalyst for the first and, more important, I focused the story on a girl named Jean with whom I myself could identify, who is in love with the boy, Ted. In a few hours, all this is changed: Ted brings a strange girl to the party and disappears into a bedroom with her, leaving Jean full of disturbing and confusing feelings. Torn between a little girl's wanting to run away and a woman's desire to know, Jean's sense of Ted's betrayal is in conflict with her feelings of having herself betrayed Ted in some way she cannot, is not yet ready to, understand.

The late critic Harry Hansen, one of the O. Henry Prize judges, who awarded me a prize the year I wrote the story, commented most favorably on my treatment of a *group's* reactions to a girl's distress. Yet at the time of the original incident I don't recall having been particularly aware of the crowd at all. Indeed, most of the characters I created had not been present at the original party, but were drawn from memories of other faces glimpsed in later years.

Occasionally stories are written from memory transformed by dreams. They are not always successful. My husband once had a dream in a hospital, from which he roused himself at 3 A.M. to write in bed, only to find later in the day that what he had written made no sense at all. However, the French author Colette, when she was thirty-one, wrote the story "Minne," about a recurring dream fantasy of sexual abduction she'd first had at the age of fourteen. The subject matter was so powerfully evoked that the story developed into a novel, then into a play; and probably Colette, no more than any other writer, could not have said where reality left off and the author's fantasy took over.

The arrangement of the parts of memory and invention becomes the substance everyone knows to be the "plot," which almost always is basic to a story. However, a plot that is unreal, specious, and simply invented is called "contrived," and not for many years has any conscientious writer wished to have his work so labeled. Indeed, so odious has this adjective become that some writers ignore the natural sequence of cause and effect and the drama of contrasts so necessary to interest us in the short story, to a point of boring the reader with an obscure "realism" which enlists him not at all.

Plot is as essential to fiction as the nerve that runs the length of a caterpillar, directing its exertions and its progress toward its destination. Plot is a means of keeping our characters in motion and holding the reader's participation to the conclusion of our story. It is also the line on which to hang suspense, curiosity, drama, behavior, and the sense of time's passing. Without plot, it is unlikely a reader would care very much about following a story through to the end.

Someone has said that plot shows the writer's ability to think in several directions at once and thus keep his story moving. It also indicates that the limits of our imagination have been extended beyond the point of known facts and events, which is the short story's important difference from reportage and journalism. Some stories are justifiably created whole from true happenings, but in the telling, the author's gift goes beyond to extract a deeper meaning from events, to circle freely around the subject so that he may use the fiction writer's privilege to judge characters he knows better than anyone else.

E. M. Forster's familiar example, "The King died, and then the Queen," is a simple accounting of two facts. It could be a journalistic note on history, and we would go on from there. However, while it is not a plot, it may suggest one to a writer with imagination and the freedom to indulge his talent, so that he might add: "The Queen was in perfect health only last week, and no doubt she would be alive today if the King's mind had not been poisoned against her by Iago." So we have another character in the play, and how did Iago poison the mind of the King who was so in love with his Queen?

Now the imagination goes in a different direction, into memory and past experiences, perhaps. The writer must try to recall some truly jealous person, tortured beyond sanity by suspicions planted in his mind by someone else. If *this* happens, he may ask himself; and if something or someone else then steps in; and if and if and if. The chain of development is much like that of an eager gossip who spares no effort to convince others that the tale being passed on is true. And so with all the plotting and conniving and lying and display of emotions before our eyes, we, the reader, will hiss Iago, suffer with Othello, and be moved to do battle for Desdemona, the beautiful innocent victim Shakespeare has brought before us. And taking simply the bare emotions in the plot, any one of us may extrapolate a hundred stories of our own by arranging the characters and events as they appear in our own minds.

Arnold Bennett stated in his *Notebooks* that he stopped writing short stories because he found that in every written story he had left behind the plot for a longer work—a novel, or a play. One may counter this by saying that many classical examples in such literature may be reduced to the simpler form of the short story by leaving out the lengthy passing of time, the multiplicity of characters, and the geographical and philosophical discursiveness a novel permits. Then again, some authors have used stories as first chapters in books, with background, characters, and basic plot essentially the same.

I myself once wrote a novel, *This Heart, This Hunter*, from a short story called "The Burning," which was about characters whose interest for me extended far beyond the short story form. The original situation and its consequences simply had to be explored further, since the questions raised were too complex and far-reaching to be resolved in a short story, even though they seemed to have ended there.

The theme was simple: juxtaposition of the seduction of Felicia, a highly protected but vulnerable young woman, by Victor, a cynical, aggressive, and basically unscrupulous older college student, with the event of a Ku Klux Klan cross-burning one night on the campus. Unknown to Felicia, Victor is the leader of the Klan, and the two strands of the story come together.

Yet the story did not end there; so I began to outline a novel of future events, to which both paths could lead. One path was the crisis in Felicia's emotions and her development from an immature girl into a woman who eventually takes matters into her own hands; the other, the expanding tragedies brought about by the irresponsible members of the Klan led by Victor, and his own downfall. Against the background of a small college town, the plot, now with time to develop, carried the two converging themes of love and evil to the end. After the murder of a preacher by the Klan because of the disturbing presence of his admitted "soul mate," and with the troubled participation of the preacher's son, Sandy, these and other minor characters took on greater importance. However, the overall theme remained the same, for the extended plot was inherent in the short story, and subsequent developments simply proceeded logically from all that went before.

If, then, a novel is a matter of the growth of characters or situations, a short story is a dramatic segment of a character's growth or life taken out of the total context. Yet each form may be said to have a plot.

16

Plot is about many things—character, imagination, irony, logic, and nearly always about the unexpected. Plot frequently surprises not only the reader, but the author as well. And a good plot is fun for everybody.

What makes a good plot? Most important is consistency and logic in mood and point of view. We do not approach light, inconsequential characters with solemnity unless our purpose is satire, or create a death scene in a mood of hilarity, unless we possess the great gifts of a Mark Twain or a Rossini. Which is not to say that deeper meanings are not to be found in comedies, or that lighter moments are not used sometimes for relief in tragic dramas. It was P. G. Wodehouse, the great humorist, who stated that the plot must determine the mood in which a story is written, not vice versa.

Plots, as said before, may come from memory, from subjective reactions to experiences (indeed, some feeling or emotion must be present in any fictional narrative), or from a provocative situation we have been told (gossip again!) or read about.

Plots may even be found in the daily news—not the big obvious stories, which already have been overdramatized, but small items which tie on to other ideas in one's mind. An illegitimate girl-child meets a father who has never known she existed. A man loses his job to his own daughter. A contest is won by the wrong man. On these bare facts you hang the embellishments of your imagination.

One small item I once came across has tantalized me for years, although I have yet to explore its possibilities. The item is this:

In a traveling circus which had been performing a longer time than usual in a county seat, a roustabout was gathering up unused wooden objects kept as replacements for the sideshows and merry-go-round —horses, chariots, and dummies—to be packed for the next move to a town some distance away. Working in the semidarkness he suddenly came upon, not a dummy, but the stiff body of a man, some time dead, obviously murdered. No one knew who he was nor had anyone seen him before, but someone had thrust him among the props carried by the circus from town to town. I still think this is a story to be written one day. Or perhaps some reader of this book can create a tragedy; a mystery; hardly a comedy, but a sympathetic re-creation of a dead man's life.

Ray Bradbury, the prolific and brilliant writer of fantasy stories, is most interesting when discussing the craft of writing and the genesis of his plots. With a mind prodigiously well stocked with ideas, he is not reluctant to share the secrets of his craft or to reveal where his story ideas come from; and the ideas are often as provocative as the stories he writes.

"Looking over my list of published short stories," he has said, "I can, almost without exception, summon up the event that caused the tale." Like many other contemporary writers, when young he found his best inspiration in the local library; but for Ray Bradbury it was with a difference. Not content simply to read and absorb the stories of the masters, he would "rove about, pulling books from shelves, reading a line here, a paragraph there, snatching, devouring, moving on." Then, as he says later, he often changed the endings of others' published works to suit himself! When he started on his own writing, he called it being "hit and run over by a short story," so excited was he by the act.

The results of Bradbury's truly fantastic imagination, which makes bizarre and startling connections from prosaic images or events, are illustrated by his story "The Beast at Forty Fathoms." Looking from his bedroom window one night, he says, he could see the outline of a roller coaster in the distance. Against the evening sky, the shape became so sinister he could believe it was something else again, something alive and threatening. And from that he wrote a story of a lighthouse keeper, who witnesses the love-violence of a sea monster!

It was Tolstoi who said a good writer is one who sees a street fight and from that is able to write an entire story. If the writer has kept himself open to the vagaries of his imagination, he may, when he witnesses such a disturbance, without staying to the end, go to his typewriter and relate his own fictional version of it. If he has decided in advance what the outcome may be, this incident could prod his writer's inventiveness into a choice among possible and interesting alternatives.

Say that on the one hand our writer has seen two men fighting with equal intensity surrounded by a crowd which, without apparent prejudice, is cheering on both of them. Or perhaps it is only cheering for one, who was robbed by the other and is now intent on punishing the crook as soundly as he can.

On the other hand, perhaps both are clever crooks who make a practice of faking a fight on crowded street corners in order to create a diversion, while a third man, or woman, not yet witnessed other than in the author's imagination, deftly circulates and robs the spectators.

Or the fight could be caused by a jealous row over a woman who, even now, may be seen and heard shouting encouragement from an upstairs window. Whatever the outcome, the reader will want to know: What will happen next? It is the characters themselves who enlist us in the end.

The author Jack Higgins has said, "I think in my early works I fell into the trap of thinking of a plot and making the characters act it out. Now I start with a concept, then create the characters and let the characters make it happen, as in real life."

However we are inspired, or from whatever source come our stories, let us be sure that we follow the logic of our characters, and pursue this consistently to the end.

Elizabeth Bowen has said a *mere* contemplative would not be a writer; for it is true a writer's contemplative moments must have some outlet for that disease of continuously observing other peoples' lives if his preoccupation with men and women, and their loves and pains and joys and defeats, won't leave him alone.

And if he also looks on the activities of his imagination as a game to be played with his own rules, then "he may as well settle with his typewriter while he is energetic enough to make it pay before he dies," wrote Whit. "And have fun in the doing of it!"

"Writing does not exclude the full life; it demands it," wrote Katherine Anne Porter, which is the best way of emphasizing, again, that our writings in the end should be the culmination of all the experiences and emotions and individuals we have known.

3

Characters

REBECCA WEST ONCE WROTE, "What I want to do when I write is to contemplate character—either by inventing my own in novels and short stories based on my own experience, or by studying character and history."

It is what each writer does, of course, for what is fiction but the study and contemplation of his own and others' idiosyncrasies, similarities, differences, errors, dreams, successes, failures, and ultimately his and their fate? Whether we explore life in the first person by interior monologue or through characters once or twice removed, it is life as it affects ourselves and others that we care to write and to read about. And it is in the short story that we can find character in the sharpest focus, in its most intense and frequently most revealing moments.

How then do we settle on the character we will construct? I say character, remembering that Seán O'Faoláin has cautioned us that any short story is made up primarily of concern for *one person* and our interest is focused on his particular section of life . . . a character, says O'Faoláin, who "will take our sympathies by storm."

"No one," said Somerset Maugham, "can create a character from pure observation; if it is to have life it must be at least in some degree a representation of himself." André Maurois puts it this way: we find our characters by means of the "unresolved chords to be found in every artist, complexes which begin to vibrate whenever a subject of matching resonance awakens them."

This "matching resonance" for me applies above all to persons I have known, individuals observed or maybe loved, or hated, through the years, who somehow "resonate" in other individuals I have met, creating composite characters never before quite witnessed upon this earth. For just as each living person is unlike any other, so must a character in fiction, in small but unmistakable ways, bear the author's signature, his own unique and complex personality. Cardboard characters copied from someone else, and cheap romances based on cliché virtues and vices are not worth writing about. Treat these, if you must, as you would grade-B movies or soap operas, which require little effort or commitment, only a lazy response for moments when life is at low ebb and sleep is just around the corner.

But trust those unresolved chords; they are the basis for characters you will create in your novels and short stories. Take as the first note in your chord a face on which you dwell, a personality which somehow interests you. It could be a glamorous woman from your childhood who seemed to glow with beauty and serenity. Add the next note, another woman who suggests the first in appearance and manner, but catch her in an off moment when she is quarrelsome with her husband and unfeeling with her child. Then add the third note with a woman whose characteristics seem at first sight to be identical with the other two until you see her becoming drunk and vulgar at a bar in a café. *Et voilà!* The whole chord is resolved and completed in your fiction writer's mind.

Norman Mailer some time ago admitted that half his fictional characters had a point of departure from somebody "real." "But up to now," he said, "I've not liked writing about people who are close to me, because they're too difficult to do. Their private reality obviously interferes with the reality one is trying to create. I prefer to

22

draw a character from someone I hardly know."

All characters do have a beginning somewhere in reality, and often enough these are persons we think we know and understand—or fail to understand and hope by the process of writing to know better.

Naturally we do best with characters from a milieu with which we are most familiar. Whit Burnett once advised, "Start early to fill the reservoir in your imagination with the possible characters you will gather along the way, and hold these for future use. When the reservoir is full, then open the gates and let it all flow into the form you have ready for it. And when you do, pour boldly!" (as Whit heard Gertrude Stein tell an ill-at-ease young man at one of her cocktail parties, when he spilled more than he poured into the glasses).

But Flaubert said, "As a writer one must be invisible yet every-where, as God in His heaven is." As a writer one must see more and concern oneself more with other humans' lives than the ordinary observer, even see similarities in disparate characters where on the surface none exists, as in Judy O'Grady and the Colonel's lady.

Marcel Proust once wrote, "It can be as intriguing for an artist to depict the manner of a queen as the behavior of a dressmaker." But he went on to argue, "High society has always been one of the *milieux* most favorable to the making of a writer who wants to observe the passions [and] tragedies in full development, first, because the principals have the time for them, and second, because a suffi-ciently rich vocabulary makes it possible for them to express them-selves."

Warren Bower, the critic, points out that Gogol elected to write chiefly about petty officials with whom he had worked; Maupassant about French prostitutes who provided diversion for him from time to time; and Chekhov about doctors and teachers whom he knew best. "The great artists of the short story have always spoken for a group incapable of speaking for themselves, doing it with power and earnestness because they feel a special sympathy with the members of that group." Chekhov himself wrote: "The writer should be not

23

the judge of his characters and their conversations, but only an unbiased witness."

There are writers like William Faulkner, whose characters appear vividly on both sides of the fence: the Snopes and Sartoris families had little in common other than proximity and geography—and sins against each other. In the powerful story "Barn Burning," the boy, Sarty (Sartoris) Snopes, is troubled by the conflict between the two worlds. While sensing that the more civilized values of the Sartoris family are the right ones to follow, at the same time he is torn by loyalty to his drunken and vengeful father, whose only means of asserting himself is by burning the barns of landowners who have provided him and his family with work and a place to live.

In the opening scene of Faulkner's story, Sarty is shown as tentative, troubled, and confused; he is also frightened. At the trial of his father for a barn-burning, the farmer who was its victim points to Sarty from the witness stand and says he wants the boy to testify. "He knows," he says. Sarty thinks the farmer means his older, bigger brother, but the farmer makes it clear he wants Sarty. "The little one. The boy," he says. Sarty, "crouching, small for his age, small and wiry like his father, in patched and faded jeans even too small for him, with straight, uncombed brown hair and eyes gray and wild as storm scud, saw the men between himself and the table part and become a lane of grim faces at the end of which he saw the Justice, a shabby, collarless, fraying man in spectacles, beckoning him." From here on, it is the boy the reader will care about.

But before Sarty has to testify, the farmer calls off the trial, and the judge orders Snopes to leave town. Coming out of the court, a boy shouts insults at Sarty's father, and the boys get in a fight, which Snopes stops, wearing his "stiff black coat, the wiry figure walking a little stiffly from where a Confederate provost's man's musket ball had taken him in the heel on a stolen horse thirty years ago."

Even in this casual description of the man, we are given further evidence of the father's character by the reference to the "stolen horse."

In the wagon, we see Sarty's mother crying, surrounded by her pitifully few possessions—the "clock inlaid with mother-of-pearl, which would not run, stopped at some fourteen minutes past two o'clock of a dead and forgotten day and time, which had been his mother's dowry," and not much else. But the character and helplessness of the mother is made clear to us, along with that of the two sisters who are "big, bovine, in a flutter of cheap ribbons" and seem to have no lives at all, as the family leaves to find another shanty on another plantation.

Yet when a place is found, and Sarty goes with his father to make themselves known, the elder Snopes deliberately wipes his feet on a cream-colored rug inside the house, where a Negro butler in a white linen coat shows his contempt. The lady of the house, Mrs. de Spain, appears.

Sarty "had never seen her like before, either—in a gray, smooth gown with lace at the throat and an apron tied in at the waist and the sleeves turned back, wiping cake or biscuit dough from her hands with a towel." Angrily she orders them to leave and take the rug with them to be cleaned. Snopes takes the rug, and next day destroys it with cheap lye.

In these brief descriptions, three characters emerge sharply. The elder Snopes we now see as a man who will do harm again when he has the opportunity; the Negro butler feels superior to Sarty's father; and the "lady of the house," a striking contrast to the boy's mother, represents grace and nourishment and civilized living.

In court again, Snopes is told to pay the plantation owner twenty bushels of corn from his first crop; and again Sarty knows his father is going to take revenge when he tells him, "Go to the barn and get that can of oil we were oiling the wagon with."

The boy runs outside, toward the stable, and he thinks, "I could run on and on and never look back, never need to see his face again. Only I can't, I can't—"

When he does finally rebel, it is too late to save the barn from burning or his father from his crime.

Here is a character developed through inner conflict, through the accumulated stresses in an adolescent boy with a growing sense of responsibility toward his father, but also toward others. Faulkner makes us understand this conflict by showing the boy in several dimensions: his weak obedience in doing as his father demands, his anxiety about the sure outcome of his father's rage, and his final strength and maturity when at the end he runs away.

Katherine Anne Porter wrote, "Get so well acquainted with your characters that they live and grow in your imagination exactly as if you saw them in the flesh; and finally tell their story with all the truth and tenderness and severity you are capable of." Truth, and tenderness, and severity: all are in this story of Faulkner's.

In Sherwood Anderson's "The Death of Mrs. Folger," we have a story in which the entire plot is no more than the character of one individual.

Mrs. Folger quite simply did not believe in life after death. Her son became a preacher, her husband and all around her believed fervently, but only Mrs. Folger and the narrator, the "I" who is the author, understood her belief that life itself is like being "a flower or a tree and a house or a dog," and that is it. Stubbornly she resisted to the end of her life the attempts of her family to change her beliefs.

Anderson first had to create a dwelling on earth for this unaccommodating character, so he places her in a suburban rooming house "beyond the college just at the edge of town, a huge old brick house, a great stretch of lawn, trees, a big barn. Some of the professors from the college lived there . . . two lawyers, both unmarried, a newspaper editor, a dentist. There must have been ten or twelve men and there were three or four women, all schoolteachers." Mrs. Folger warns the young narrator against one of them, because she is afraid he will fall in love with a woman older than himself. This is the only diversion from the basic theme.

The story takes final shape one night when Mrs. Folger invites the narrator to her room and asks if he believes in heaven and life after death. Not yet having heard her views, the young man apologetically says he is afraid he does not; and thus they become friends. Mrs. Folger finally dies, a strong character remaining consistent in her beliefs to the end in this absorbing and warmly evoked story of a small-town woman.

And so it goes. If you are an American—or French or English or Italian, maybe—and have ever lived in a small community, it is very likely that you know a lot of people like Mrs. Folger whose stories you would like to tell. Because you will have observed your neighbors in proximity and remembered them, it will not be hard to put them into a story in situations which you will imagine for them.

And here we come again to the matter of gossip, and to my conviction that the real origin of the short story goes very far back in time to our almost universal love of the tales told about our neighbors and acquaintances, friends or foes, in small towns and cities as well. Remember *The Canterbury Tales,* and Boccaccio's wicked accounts of respectable persons in church and state who were not what they seemed; and consider our continued fascination with the lives and loves of actresses, politicians, and even former presidents' wives —our fascination is with the appearances and revelations of the individuals themselves.

In journalistic writing, our written words had better be verifiable, or we will find ourselves in legal trouble. But in fiction, we have no obligation to get the facts straight, only to present the character and the essence of *truth* as we see it, or imagine it, and take off from there. How our story will come out then will be dictated by the degree of our sympathy or understanding, our condemnation of or outrage at events, and the play of our imagination. Maybe we will even write our story simply in order to *find out* the deeper truth hidden in a situation—as Robert Frost once remarked, "to see what I feel."

Of course, in fictional "honesty," we may embellish or even distort the obvious, since our imaginations also will be at work with our subconscious or intuition, eager to inform us beyond the facts.

Let us, for example, take an ex-senator's wife who has long been suspected of being an alcoholic. It has never been quite known if she

27

took the cure, or if she really did spend weeks at a time at a famous beauty farm, losing weight. Gossip abounds: she was seen at an official dinner, making incredibly silly remarks; she is interviewed on television and her hands shake uncontrollably, cruelly caught by the camera; she has had several bad falls, and once at a state dinner it was noticed that her upper arms were mysteriously covered with bruises.

So the possibilities for fiction here go beyond known facts, and further development may reach out in any direction the author wishes. Whether the fictional character is to be treated sympathetically or is to be condemned is the writer's prerogative; perhaps he will decide none of the gossip has been true, but that it was simply fabricated by some clever politician of a rival party. This then could be the story in itself, an injustice done to an innocent victim.

The chances are, of course, that this is one story which editors would reject, since the conclusion of a character's blamelessness can only be slick fiction if it ends in a false happy ending, and less than convincing if it ends in undiluted tragedy. But would it be so "slick" after all? Couldn't one see the ex-senator's wife as a universal and tragic figure, a woman who has been carried along beyond her own capacities and imagination into a kind of quicksand from which she cannot free herself? Or a woman who is envious of her husband's success, perhaps, and jealous of his effect on others, particularly women; who is, in effect, subconsciously hoping to bring disgrace on him by her own actions? Yet who is nonetheless a tragic figure out of her place and time, who cannot save even herself?

In such a story, there would be many small climaxes, based on the wife's character alone; and in order to make her convincing, one would have to pinpoint her speech, her appearance, and her effect on others. We would have to create a character that the reader would believe is unique, a character who would be confused with no one else, whose name could never be borne by another.

Here, now, we come to another element in creating characters—choice of names. "Life begins with the age of names," wrote André

Maurois, and surely any living person would feel unclothed, certainly anonymous if his name was taken from him. Yet not many of us may choose our own; certainly for the writer, not every name seems the only name possible for the character it is attached to. Writers have even been known to change names midstream as actions and habits and directions evolve in the process of writing. The American Johns, Marys, and Susans may, on our story's development, seem not to apply to more foreign traits written into our character or the story.

Fancy names of course are out. They belong primarily in soap operas, where the viewer must make quick identification of the characters so hastily dramatized before him. Names like von Rockefeller to show excessive wealth, Mary Jane to show sweetness and goodheartedness, Butch to show toughness—you can do better than that.

Scorn it or not, one way to find a name is to read your telephone book, especially if you are in another town or country. And if you lack the inspiration to give your character a name which will become unmistakably his or her own, then try out a whole list of names. Very likely there is only one which will really suit, and when this comes to you, you'll be agreeably surprised.

Names must also fit into the background of your story. A Catholic girl may be called Mary; but not a Jewish girl, who may be Miriam. If a boy called John is English, in Austria he will be Johannes. These facts are obvious. The important thing is to find appropriate names for your characters—from your own memory if possible. Settle on the one which comes closest to suiting its would-be owner, or your own feeling of familiarity with the character.

Character development is, of course, tied to the point of view you have adopted for your story. If you tell it from the mind of one of the characters, your task would seem easy—you concentrate on that one person's thoughts and feelings. Conveying a sense of character would seem especially easy if you tell the story as if the person were yourself. After all, we know ourselves best. Ivy Compton-Burnett observed, "I believe we know much less of others than we think, that it would be a great shock to find oneself suddenly behind another person's eyes."

Yet an objective approach in the third person may permit greater latitude in approaching other characters' minds and intentions. An "I" narrator cannot see everywhere, except by hearsay; once removed, or twice, you may cover several points of view, including the omniscient, in your story line.

No matter what the point of view, before we begin to write about a character, any character, including our own, we must dig into motivations and *raisons d'être* with the same fervor as a dog after a bone he finds buried just beyond his reach. Obsession, again, but in focus; in building a character we must concentrate all we know about him into the telling, so that at our story's end the reader will feel that no other interpretation than we provide was possible.

And in order to do this we must, as Alfred Kazin once wrote of Sinclair Lewis, "move creatively in the channels of the character we have created."

T. S. Eliot observed, "I think of character and dialogue, and extend it to design."

Of tremendous importance to the reader is dialogue, speech, the sounds we make that distinguish us from other mammals and from one another. Speak aloud your written dialogue in the characters' voices, intone the rhythm of your speech as would an actor on stage. Feel how words may be combined to communicate or to conceal, to show love, passion, doubt, distrust, or simple friendship. As in a foreign language, *where* the stress comes in a word or in a sentence is particularly important. Observe carefully at which part of the sentence you must somehow so arrange the words of your dialogue that they sound as only you know them to sound, since you have listened carefully as they are spoken in your own mind.

Also, in dialogue, allow for pauses and hesitations, slashing out with a ruthless pen excess wordage, too slow beginnings, stiffness, self-consciousness, and phoniness.

Here are a few short sentences which may help in your character-building and add to your technique:

1. You may add credence and vividness to your character's appearances or validity by having other characters speak well, or ill, or affectionately, or scornfully, of him before he is even on the scene. Or after.
2. Stand outside your character and look in; crawl inside your character and *be* him.
3. Look for your character's reactions and justifications in your own behavior; try to find any similar faults, virtues, or habits in embryo inside yourself and try to understand them fully. Even to condemn them!
4. Practice this trick of the imagination: visualize the facial characteristics of one person on the body of another; give the dress of one woman to the figure of another. Give children to a childless woman, and see how this affects her personality. Watch the tragedy of one who has lost those she most cares about, one who is now deprived, after having always been treated to the best of everything.

And remember, above all, that the short story is about men and women—and dogs and cats and birds and bees, if you will, as well as children—and the more patient your research and the more loving your attention, the better your fiction will be.

Trollope said, "On the last day of each month recorded, every person in a work of fiction should be a month older than on the first." We go with our characters wherever they lead us, and as time makes its mark on us, so it must on them.

4

Style

STYLE, said Robert Louis Stevenson, is the foundation of the art of literature. "Style is a matter of finding out who you are, and then presenting yourself to the world," wrote the English critic, Quentin Crisp. "And to say what you have to say, no matter what the question."

"To write is to reveal oneself," warns André Maurois, which, as a matter of fact, is precisely that which a young writer most fears. But this is what he must accept, as early as his writing ambition begins to unfold.

Katherine Anne Porter wrote, "If you have a character of your own, you will have a style of your own. . . . Your style grows as your ideas grow, and as your knowledge of your craft increases." And as your knowledge of your craft grows, the reading you have done and the observations you have accumulated and absorbed from life itself will begin to be sorted out in your mind in tune to a rhythm which is your own. It is from this point on that anything and everything become part of your "style."

Whit Burnett, who devoted his life to the art of the short story, thought a great deal about style, recognizing it early on in young writers, respecting its originality, encouraging its development, and emphasizing it as one of the most essential elements in any writer's bag of talents. Yet, "The best style is the *least* noticeable," he wrote. "And the very best is that which least stands in the way of the material presented."

In *STORY* Magazine, which we edited together for so long, the "story" comes first, we said. Yet on analyzing the more than two thousand stories appearing during the magazine's forty years of publication, it became clear that few stories succeeded in the eyes of the editors, or the readers, without bearing the coloration of the author's individuality, his personal and unique point of view: his style. Even though he might have written with strict objectivity, the rhythm of his speech and thought patterns—in other words, the personal style in his writing—had to make its impression first on the reader's mind.

Then what is style, that it appears in so many different guises to so many disparate writers? When and how does one develop one's own, and how can we know we are not, in Professor Riley Hughes's words, being "grammatically correct in English and yet stylistically deadly"?

E. B. White wrote some years ago, "There is no satisfactory example of style, no infallible guide to good writing, no assurances that a person who thinks clearly will be able to write clearly, no key that unlocks the door, no inflexible rules by which a young writer may shape his course." He continued, "The beginner should approach style warily, realizing that it is himself he is approaching; no other."

There is no "right" style and no style is "wrong." There is only that style which fits your own personality and beliefs and heartbeat. As to how a story is to be told, its scope and its point of view, it will do you no good to consider any tastes or ears other than your own if you expect to develop to the full your potential individuality, which *is* style.

In both writing and reading, the ear as well as the eye will be at work. We do not only place words on a page, we also hear them, the sense, the cadence, and the emotional vibrations. All our senses must

33

be stirred by our unique and creative susceptibilities: words, written or spoken, do reverberate in the mind.

"A writer must so train his ear that he shall be able to weigh the rhythm of every word as it falls from his pen," Anthony Trollope wrote long ago. "The habit of writing well comes to the writer who is a severe critic to himself. Harmony comes from practice of the ear."

A writer, a critic, and an editor all must acknowledge that there are as many styles as there are writers in the short story form. Over the years, we found that each story we printed had a different master. Through the Depression years, the Nazi and Fascist eras, through World War II and Homecoming, the Korean and Vietnam wars, into the Beat generation, and just touching on the current trends in science fiction and the use of short stories on television, we, at *STORY*, were interested and receptive to them all.

In the 1930s, William Saroyan's "Daring Young Man on the Flying Trapeze" had an impact that affected the styles of many young writers victimized by the Depression. His stories, written in a manner hyperbolically his own and sharply tuned to the drums of his own personality, seemed fresh and newly born onto the American scene.

He wrote how his character (always Saroyan himself) "walked into the day as alertly as might be, making a definite noise with his heels, perceiving with his eyes the superficial truth of street and structures, the trivial truth of reality. Helplessly, his mind sang *He Flies Through the Air with the Greatest of Ease, This Daring Young Man on the Flying Trapeze,* then laughed with all the might of his being."

No one quite knew what that famous story was about, but readers felt an emotional response to Saroyan's *joie de vivre* and style that was strong enough to set the young man on his impressive career.

Let it be said he, like all of us, owed much to writers of earlier generations who had already broken through barriers and were expressing themselves in the short story form with renewed vitality. Saroyan's freedom of association was made easier by the originality of Gertrude Stein, the iconoclasm of James Joyce, and the simplicity of Sherwood Anderson, whose impact on American short story writers was immediate. Even so, Saroyan's style was his own—open-hearted and wide-eyed, his unshackled imagination expressing vitality and native eloquence. Unfortunately, as he grew older, and his life experiences made him bitter about the world and its occupants, his achievements seemed to freeze in his earlier fame, so that Henry Miller wrote that Saroyan's "evolution is not in the direction one would imagine. He took a big hurdle in the beginning, but he refuses to go on hurdling. He is running now and his stride is pleasant and easy, but we had expected him to be a chamois and not a yearling."

Still, Saroyan did become important on the literary scene by realizing early on that it was "himself he was approaching; no other," and recording this in his own unique fictional style.

A writer whose best stories are as modern today as in the 1930s is Kay Boyle. Her "Rest Cure" was a *tour de force* on a theme not always successfully brought off: Young-Artist-Meets-Old-Artist, the young writer registering that meeting with intense participation and sensitivity. It is a theme which has been done (recently in Philip Roth's *The Ghost Writer*) nearly to death but seldom so well. Boyle's style, observant and gently ironic, was perfectly attuned to the subject and the mood of a dying genius on his last days in sunny Italy.

In her story, the older writer, based on D. H. Lawrence, is sitting in the sun with a blanket wrapped around him and his hands "lying like emaciated strangers before him." He is angry, passionate, and still caring. In his invalid's petulance he is fretfully hoping that "today the sun would survive, until the trees below the terrace effaced it toward four o'clock, like opened parasols." On the railing before him, the parched stems of dying geraniums "bore their soiled white flowers balanced upon their thick Italian heads like a row of weary washerwomen leaning from a villainous descent of the coast."

Brooding, because his wife is chatting indoors with a visiting editor, the writer recalls his dead father, a miner, remembering how the black of the pits had put "some kind of blasphemy on his own blood."

His wife comes out with the editor, whose "solid gray head seemed to cork the sunlight." They have brought the invalid a gift of a live lobster.

The invalid protests, irritably, that he can't bear them alive, and tension rises in the scene among the three of them—until the wife goes back in the house and returns with a bottle of chilled champagne.

She opens it as he watches her: "A great strong woman whom he would never forget, never, nor the surprisingly slim crescent of her flexible thumbs," he thinks as he lies there.

The cork flies out and hits the visiting publisher on the forehead; quickly the mood of the invalid changes. "A sweet shy look of love had begun to arch in his eyes." He even asks to hold the *langouste* —but then again his good humor vanishes as he identifies it with his dead father. At the end, in his depression, he whispers, "Father, Father, I don't want to die," as his fingers close for comfort about the body of the *langouste*.

So perfectly structured is the whole of this slight but many-layered story that it could well serve as a model for interdependence of style and matter in the hands of a master craftswoman.

Another story, in another style, has long been the trademark of Jesse Stuart. His stories of ordinary people in Kentucky have become classics, although writing in this genre can be tricky, depending as it does on anecdote, skilled dialogue, and credibility. In Stuart's case the style is indigenous to his own humorous and balanced view of life and passes without a single false note. Such distortions as he uses are essential to the tale, and treated so truthfully that inflection, as well as spelling, make the dialogue ring true in our ears.

In "Clothes Make the Man," we read about the friends, Eig and Bergis, whose job it is to chop down trees for the sawmill crowd working in the valley below. Bergis tells the story, of how his friend Eig suddenly goes wild, beating his chest and yelling "like a lonesome wildcat among the mountain cliffs. And he really looked wild."

Looking down on the road below, where many cars are passing, Eig begins taking off all his clothes and beating his chest with his "big fire-shovel hand," letting out yells which echo from the distant rocks across the valley. "The calves of his muscular legs were like gnarled tree roots, his long feet were like sled runners, and his ankles and big toes were woolly. I had seen many lumberjacks stripped, but I'd never seen one so woolly as Eig."

"Wonder if they've ever seen a wild man in these parts?" Eig yells at Bergis, and grabbing up the bleached bone of a dead animal they'd found in the woods, he goes tearing off down to the highway, vowing to "skeer the wits outen 'em!"

Which he does. Bergis can see the cars below stop and excited men jump out shouting, some with guns to shoot wildly at the naked woolly figure running toward them.

Luckily just as the sheriff arrives with his deputies, Eig races back up the mountain, managing to get his clothes back on while Bergis hides the big bone.

Not suspecting Eig's tricks, the sheriff tells both Bergis and Eig to carry guns from now on to protect themselves from the wild man. Next day the papers are filled with the story. Eig has fooled everyone. But when the excitement dies down Eig still isn't satisfied and tells Bergis he's got to "stir 'em up again, before the timber gets too green."

Once more Eig sheds his clothes, takes up the bone, and runs down the mountain to the highway. Again the motorists panic, again the wild shooting from men in cars. But on this occasion Eig doesn't get back up the mountain in time to put on his clothes before the sheriff and his men close in.

Still Eig has the presence of mind to yell,

" 'Did you see 'im?'

" 'See who?'

" 'That damned wild man!' " says Eig, who then claims to have been robbed of his clothes and "flailed" over his head with a big bone. The story gets around, and now everybody in town is laughing at Eig—for not carrying his gun like the rest of them and for letting himself get victimized like that.

37

So here again we have a style perfectly suited to the author's unique sense of storytelling, this time on the American scene.

A rule given by E. B. White in *The Elements of Style*, that indispensable small volume written by White and William Strunk, Jr., states, "Before beginning to compose something, gauge the nature and extent of the enterprise and work from a suitable design. Design informs even the simplest structure, whether of brick and steel or of prose."

"Indeed, where form is lacking, the idea no longer exists," said Gustave Flaubert years ago. Yet now, to quote Hortense Calisher in her fine introduction to *The Best American Short Stories 1981*, many short story writers are "expending their main juices in antic buzzing between 'fact' and 'fiction,' " by throwing the "dilemma" of the story "straight back into the lap of the hopefully dissective reader, who may not thank you for it unless he or she has been reading the same dogma as you."

This is pertinent to our subject: today there are writers who seem to approach fiction with no apparent "design" at all. The critic Bernard Blackstone says, "Approaching the raw material of his age too closely, the writer of talent, rather than genius, is sucked into the whirlpool and lost. Lost, that is, as an artist." Though he records facts, experiences, and observations with sharp visual awareness, even a touch of poetry, still the author's intention and the category in which he sees himself leaves one hard put to understand why he has not written in some form other than the short story.

"Brownstone," an O. Henry Prize winner by Renata Adler, is a story with little relevance to E. B. White's dictum, which goes further: "A writer cannot plunge in blindly and (simply) start ticking off fact after fact about his man, lest he miss the forest for the trees and there be no end to his labors." And "even the kind of writing that is essentially adventurous and impetuous will on examination be found to have a secret plan."

"Brownstone" has no discernible plan as it opens in a flight of fancy not unlike Saroyan's, but Saroyan's events followed some logic in a celebration of life. Adler's do not seem related at all to what follows: "The Apollo flight, the four-minute mile, Venus in Scorpio, human records on land and at sea, these have been events of enormous importance."

This means, I suppose, that what follows has little importance as the character tells about herself. She is a young woman who goes to a lot of parties, who hears gossip about her neighbors—one from across the hall, a couple on the third floor who "play Bartok on their stereo," and a girl on the fourth floor. There is also mentioned a murdered landlord, which fact seems to have no importance either.

We go with the author to a dog pound where she fancies a quarrelsome St. Bernard, and takes him for a walk; this too comes to nothing.

Next, a long reminiscence about a cousin who is a veterinarian; a conversation with a cab driver whom she does not tip. Then there is Aldo, "who lives with me between the times he prefers to be alone."

We go to another party, then get a tedious reminiscence about her college days; there is another reference to the murdered landlord, unmourned and almost forgotten, and so on and on and on again, back to "Aldo" in Los Angeles.

The style here is as undemanding as good dinner-table conversation among guests who do not expect ever to see one another again, nor do they care to. Example: "My cousin is well. The problem is this. Hardly anyone about whom I deeply care at all resembles anyone else I have ever met, or heard of, or read about in literature. I know an Israeli general who, in 1967, retook the Mitla Pass but who, since his mandatory retirement from military service at fifty-five, has been trying to repopulate the Ark. He asked me, over breakfast at the Drake, whether I know any owners of oryxes."

As you can see, Adler would make an amusing guest at a dinner party, or better yet on a TV talk show. But is this a story?

It is true the form of the short story has become increasingly flexible in recent decades, and successful experiments may present something almost new in a writer's sensory approach to his subject.

Joyce Carol Oates's "The Dead," like Adler's "Brownstone," is a story about relationships in our time. Presented with depth and emotion, it is equally adventurous in style, reflecting, to quote Anatole Broyard, "the language of emergency, of anxiety, of finality." Generationally and experientially, "The Dead" succeeds in making fictional art from a girl's equally subjective life-style and affairs of the heart.

This young woman, married when the story begins, swallows pills for unhappiness, pills for insomnia, amphetamines to speed herself up. She has a married lover, Gordon, and she also inspires devotion in the heart of a neurotic and sensitive fellow student, Emmett, without realizing the intensity of his infatuation until it is too late. We *see* this girl: "Her copper-colored hair fell in a jumble about her face, and her skin sometimes took a radiant coppery beauty from the late afternoon sun as it sheered mistily through the campus trees, or from the excitement of a rare good class and from the thought of her love for Gordon, who would be waiting to see her after class."

There is a crisis and the girl goes away: Gordon returns to his wife. The young woman writes a book which sells well. She is divorced, and she takes another lover in another town; she does not forget Gordon. When she is invited to lecture at the old college, at a party in her honor she is shocked to hear of the suicide of the student, Emmett, who loved her.

Gordon is at the party, and they leave and go to her room, as in the past. But when they make love she suddenly sees her former husband's face before her with a look of surprise and shock, "as though she had betrayed him." Then his face blends with the face of Emmett, the dead student, and Gordon's face "pressed so close to her in the dark she could not see it. The bed was crammed with people.

" 'Do you want me to leave?' Gordon asked.

"She could not speak."

And so the story ends in a certain hopelessness which seems to the reader not unfaithful to the world we live in; there is an effective and plausible pattern in this story of a girl unable to find her way in her emotions or in her love life. The reader wants to know how the meeting with Gordon will work out and how the story will end. One cares. Oates, without trickery or sentimentality, lets us share her knowledge of the stages of contemporary love, and a woman's growing acceptance of inevitable endings in life. Nor would this story be so successful without the reader's sense that the author knows intuitively the effect she is creating and intends to leave with the reader.

Many writers when dealing with the emotions fall into clichés or show insincerity, or even voyeurism; yet the best writers of our time have written memorably about the emotions, about relations between the sexes, about love and death. For them it has not been enough to simply record happenings. The complexities of D. H. Lawrence, the sophistication and fatalism of Hemingway, the playful candor of Henry Miller, and the associational tricks of James Joyce all express these writers' stylistic uniqueness among their peers.

Take "The Fox" by D. H. Lawrence, which tells of two women living together on a farm during the First World War. "Banford, though nervous and delicate, has a warm, generous soul; March, though so odd and absent in herself, had a strange magnanimity. Yet in the long solitude, they were apt to become irritable with one another, tired of one another."

Both women hope to kill the fox that is destroying their chickens; yet one day March was unable to fire when she "suddenly saw the fox. He was looking up at her. His chin was pressed down, and his eyes were looking up. They met her eyes. And he knew her."

Then: "He was gone, softly, soft as the wind." March follows him with her gun, determined to find him, but the reader knows she will not shoot him.

The months pass, until one night the women hear a voice at the door and a young man comes in. March, almost at once, comes under the influence of his "strange, soft, modulated voice," when he explains that this house had been his home five years before; now he has no place to go. The girls decide to let him stay awhile, but "suddenly he lifted his clouded blue eyes, and, unthinking, looked straight into March's eyes. He was startled as well as she. He, too, recoiled a little. March felt the same sly taunting knowing spark leap out of his eyes as he turned his head aside and fall into her soul, as it had fallen from the dark eyes of the fox."

Banford furiously fights the attraction between March and the boy, even when he kills the fox for them late one night, and hangs it in the shed for them to see.

"It was a lovely dog-fox in its prime with a handsome thick winter coat: a lovely golden-red color, grey as it passed to the belly, and belly all white, and a great full brush with a delicate black and grey and pure white tip."

The tension among the three individuals mounts as March becomes more helplessly responsive to the boy. The night before he departs for Canada, he manages to draw her outdoors, leaving Banford in tears.

" 'Isn't my heart as good as her heart?' " he asks, and with his hot grasp he takes March's hand and presses it under his left breast. " 'There's my heart,' he said. 'If you don't believe in it.' "

And then "she felt the deep, heavy, powerful stroke of his heart, trembling like something from beyond. It was like something from beyond, something awful from outside, signaling to her. And the signal paralyzed her. It beat upon her soul and made her helpless. She forgot Jill [Banford]. She could not think of Jill any more."

When the boy goes back to Canada, Banford seems to have won, until he returns and finds the two women outside beside a tree which must be cut down. He offers to do this in spite of Banford's antagonism.

But "in his heart he had decided her death. A terrible still force seemed in him, and a power that was just his."

" 'Mind yourself, Miss Banford,' " he warns, standing there with the axe in his hand. But she refuses to move.

"There was a moment of pure, motionless suspense when the world seemed to stand still. Then suddenly his form seemed to flash up enormously tall and fearful, he gave two swift, flashing blows, in immediate succession, the tree severed, turning slowly, spinning strangely in the air and coming down like a sudden darkness on the earth. No one saw what was happening except himself. No one heard the strange little cry which Banford gave as the dark end of the bough swooped down, down on her. No one saw her crouch a little and receive the blow on the back of the neck. No one saw her flung outwards and laid, a little twiching heap, at the foot of the fence. No one except the boy. And he watched with intense bright eyes, as he would watch a wild goose he had shot. Was it winged? Or dead?"

March was staring at the sea's horizon "as if it were not real." Then she looked around at him "with the strained, strange look of a child that is struggling against sleep," not understanding that Banford was dead.

It is in writing of the emotions that style becomes most individual, in moments of passion, of betrayal, of life and death. Hemingway, whose own emotional scenes stripped of nonessentials showed the way for many writers to reach into the far corners of their experiences, has said such writing must be "without tricks and without cheating." Hemingway gives us no sense we are being cheated, no fear that he is holding back all that a writer is supposed to know and reveal. "No faking," he said.

Archibald MacLeish stated that in Hemingway "we have the one intrinsic style our country has produced." In a frequently anthologized Hemingway story, "The Snows of Kilimanjaro," we read about the last days of a writer on safari in Africa with his wife, after his leg has been injured and gangrene has set in. In this passage, Harry has become delirious, and the style is uniquely Hemingway's own:

> Just then, death had come and rested its head on the foot of the cot and he could smell its breath.
> "Never believe any of that about a scythe and skull," he told his

wife. "It can be two bicycle policemen as easily, or be a bird. Or it can have a wide snout like a hyena."

It had moved up on him now, but it had no shape any more. It simply occupied space.

"Tell it to go away."

It did not go away, but moved a little closer.

"You've got a hell of a breath," he told it. "You stinking bastard."

It moved up closer to him still, and he could not speak to it, and when it saw he could not, it came a little closer, and now he tried to send it away without speaking, but it moved in on him so its weight was all upon his chest, and while it crouched there and he could not move, or speak, he heard the woman say, "Bwana is asleep. Take the cot up very gently and carry it into the tent."

John Gunther wrote, "Even the most insignificant words or phrases can assist or destroy the cadence and euphony of a style."

And Harold Pinter once said in an interview that a writer must feel every sentence to be a nugget. "You should be able to hold it in your hand . . . and say it exists, it's paying for its keep, it is essential." Hemingway's dialogue is like that.

Above all, a writer must develop a feeling for the power and the diversity of dialogue, the style of spoken words. Entire stories have been built on speech, as is the one by Donald Barthelme which, says his publisher, is "stripped of everything save voices."

"On the Steps of the Conservatory" is about a meeting between two music students, one, Hilda, who has just been rejected by the admissions committee, and the other, Maggie, who is an accepted student and rather smug about it. Hilda's distress is apparent in the opening pages of the story and continues until Maggie says falsely:

—Well Hilda there are other things in life.

—Yes Maggie I suppose there are. None that I want.

—Non-Conservatory people have their own lives. We Conservatory people don't have much to do with them but we are told they have their own lives.

—I suppose I could file an appeal if there's anywhere to file an appeal to. If there's anywhere.

—That's an idea. We get stacks of appeals, stacks and stacks.

—I can wait all night. Here on the steps.

—I'll sit with you. I'll help you formulate the words.

—Are they looking out of the window?

—Yes I think so. What do you want to say?

—I want to say my whole life depends on it. Something like that.

—It's against the rule for Conservatory people to help non-Conservatory people you know that.

—Well Goddammit I thought you were going to help me!

In the end the girls part, Maggie saying smugly that "time heals everything."

This *is* a story, slight and almost unpunctuated though it is, with a vivid use of dialogue. It has characters, a dilemma which is or is not going to be solved, the rise and fall of dramatic emphasis, and a conclusion which yet leaves us involved beyond the time covered.

Briefly now, let us consider punctuation, which also is essentially part of style but not always understood by fiction writers. We know to place a period at the end of a complete sentence; a semicolon if another related sentence seems to vary the thought, as in a paradox, or in order to add other subjects in the same vein.

An independent quotation in the body of a sentence is enclosed in quotation marks with all punctuation except the comma or period *out*side; dialogue is enclosed in quotation marks, with the punctuation *within* the final quote.

We use quotation marks around dialogue or titles, but never around the *thoughts* of characters. The contradiction works in the Hemingway story, only because Harry's delirium gives reality to the imaginary object he actually believes to be there.

Many writers spend much of their rewriting time putting in commas, semicolons, and then taking these out again. Oscar Wilde once complained, "I was working on the proof of one of my poems all the morning, and took out a comma. In the afternoon I put it back again."

"No iron can pierce the heart with such force as a period put just at the right place," says the narrator in Isaac Babel's short story "Guy de Maupassant." And indeed, this too is a matter of the style of an author.

Dots, or ellipses, we may use at the end of a sentence or in dialogue if the speaker's voice trails off, leaving a thought incomplete. And we use dashes after a clause—on the typewriter two hyphens, never just one—to make a parenthetical thought related to the sentence.

Finally, do not carry your metaphors to excess or you will end with something like those which came to us now and then at *STORY* Magazine.

"He placed his megalocephalous hands on her wilderness of breasts."

"It was all she had of him—a shell, waiting for a hook-up."

In conclusion, *what happens* in the short story is above all the main consideration. The single most important result of a successful style is to render more effective and compelling the truth we wish to relate. Prose style is not poetry; in fact, Manuel Komroff, the novelist and short story writer, once said that when he found his prose fiction acquiring somehow the rhythm of a poem, he cut it off at once. That made it "too easy" he said; it wasn't what prose was meant to do.

Anatole Broyard points out that language from which style is created requires not the usage of uncommon words, but "using them uncommonly well." And he reminds us that T. S. Eliot, when lecturing at Harvard, "used to pause for as much as five minutes while seeking exactly the word he wanted."

Broyard also repeats another observation, which particularly appeals to me: "A cliché begins as heartfelt, and then its heart sinks." Clichés are too frequently used but cannot be ignored. My own advice to young writers has always been, "A cliché, like an insult, should only be used intentionally."

The important thing about style is simply to write as well as one is able, to give thought to each word and to weigh each one spoken or written for its true sense, its effectiveness, and its color; to read the best of the older writers as well as the clearest and most modern of one's contemporaries, pausing frequently as over a gourmet meal.

And above all to take pleasure and pride in our vocabulary, that language we have had handed down to us from all those centuries of erudition and experiment and passion—the greatest gift of all, on whose use absolutely no limitations have been placed other than proper respect for its rules.

A final definition by the critic Sidney Cox: "Style is the effectual working of the point of view. It is the grace given by a free imagination. It is of your unexamined depths and all of you. And when all of you is centered—with no part standing off to criticize, admire, or guide—no wonder you show what you did not know you had, and act with style."

5

Work and the Writer

J. P. Marquand described his work habits this way: "I sit around and think about it. The more leisure and freedom a writer has to sit around and think about his work the better. The physical business of writing is secondary to contemplation."

Yes and no. *Thinking* isn't work for the writer, it's what he does best; "applying the seat of the pants to the seat of the chair," as the Nobel Prize–winning author Sinclair Lewis once advised, is harder, but a habit to cultivate if we would reach our goal.

Working habits, of course, are different for each writer. Some of these are interesting to read about; some are absurdly trivial. My writing husband and I had solemn arguments about his preferring to write with his back to the light, and I to working with an uncluttered window before me, preferably facing trees and bushes moving with a breeze. Our son works best on a rocking sailboat with the bay around him. Hemingway is said to have worked standing up, while Proust wrote his wonderful prose in bed.

So the hours when one works are always an individual matter. Don Robertson, a former newspaper reporter, worked the night away at his novels and short stories, but Mary O'Hara, who wrote the

"Flicka" books, said she simply rises earlier and earlier each morning until finally she is at her typewriter before darkness has lifted. Balzac, whose creativity spurred him on both night and day, worked best after short periods of sleep at odd and unusual hours, ignoring all family and social life. While surviving on something like fifty cups of coffee a day, he kept his energies totally focused on writing—until a work was done, when he released his tensions in excessive and reckless dissipations. Unfortunately, he died young!

You, the writer, may well ask yourself, What are my most effective hours of work in the life I lead? What part of each day do I usually sit, productively, at my typewriter? When is the flow of thoughts and words and ideas least impeded by external interruptions? Do I work best in the morning, afternoon, or all night until dawn? Seated upright, or reclining in a bed? With pen in hand, or rigidly at a typewriter, or even a word processor?

It is foolish, of course, to think that imitating the work habits of any other writer will automatically produce one's own best work, yet there is no harm in asking certain questions of oneself if one would make the most of those periods of greatest energy and creativity. Each of us does vary strikingly in alertness and productivity at certain periods of our working days, and this fact does have significance for the work we do best. Almost from birth we are all either morning persons or nightowls (or there would be fewer listeners to late-night talk shows!). We even recognize in our children those who are naturally early risers and those who are not.

As for other factors which influence the rhythm and effectiveness of our lives and the work we do, well-known studies in "body time" have measured our energies and responses to a change in time zones, for example. Even the direction in which we fly makes a difference in the degree of fatigue we feel at the end of a journey by plane, and some researchers have claimed that traveling from east to west causes greater exhaustion at the end of a trip than traveling from west to east. In earlier days, when one crossed oceans by ship rather than by plane, the sea was said to stimulate a writer's creativity—but no writer yet has claimed to create more effectively on a plane's crossing. Are we most stimulated by being constantly surrounded by people? What effect does isolation have on us? In a *New York Times'* reported study of a human subject kept in isolation thirty days in a windowless room, the subject's perception of time changed abruptly and dramatically once she was separated from the outside world; her sleeping hours and also her sense of focus became other than they had been.

And an astrologer will tell you that your energies are most concentrated each day at the hour at which you were born!

Facts or fantasies, you will do well to mark your own rhythms early in your writing life, to take advantage of those times when your energies are greatest, when your mental and imaginative activities are sharpest and brightest.

Unfortunately, freedom of choice in writing time is not always available. Even Henry James could complain about "the much life and the little art" as circumstances, too often, prevented him from obeying the writing impulse at the moment of inspiration.

It would be helpful indeed if writers could synchronize their creative clocks with all the other demands made on their lives—but students have class hours. A mother has obligations to home and family. A job imposes its own hourly restrictions; and the professional in any field may be on call at hours of the day or night not of his own choosing.

Does one wait for inspiration before starting to write? For lightning to strike one with an idea? "No," says Katherine Anne Porter, a sensible analyst of the writer's habits and impulses and achievements. She says that a writer does not wait for inspiration: "He works at it!" Because, she goes on to say, "Writing isn't an elegant pastime." It is not just something that happens, painlessly. "It is a sober and hard-worked trade."

Nevertheless, inspiration is a very fine thing and should be cultivated so far as it is possible. For when it directs our pen we write faster, eliminate false starts and uncertainties, and find ourselves more firmly committed to the idea, the mood, or our characters with a certainty that a story is there within our reach, perhaps even hovering overhead ready (almost) to write itself.

Also, a certain encouraging mental process takes place once the decision to write a story is made. Then, if the basic idea has vitality and wit and strength of narrative, other provocative and essential facts or fantasies begin to accrete around it. Stendhal's famous analogy—likening transformation by human love to a bare branch dipped in the salt mines of Silesia: a dazzling and beautiful crystallization takes place in the loved one—shows us the process by which a writer may dip a story idea into his imagination so that facets unsuspected before reflect back beauties and significances beyond the first bare reality.

Once the idea is glittering in your mind with all the possibilities and layers of interpretation your imagination is imparting to it, and once the time for work is set aside, you are committed to work.

Chekhov wrote: "When the wings of my mind are beating, I've got to go ahead!"

And, Erskine Caldwell has said: "Writing is as habit-forming as tobacco."

In the writing game, your chief opponent is not the critics you will face, your friends, publisher, or even the limited time you can give to your typewriter. Unfortunately it is you, yourself—your own sometimes reluctant imagination, your inevitable questioning of the value of time spent, or, too often, a lack of confidence that you will be successful in communicating to a reader all that is in your mind. You must write with an authority you may not feel, cross all boundaries between the idea and its execution without a hitch. And there are no simple guidelines to show you your way.

Even your imagination must often be outmaneuvered and forced to obey your orders—but not too rigidly, not with too much calculated thought. You must give your dream—for that in essence is what a short story is—its head, let it lead you to that reader whom now you think of not as an opponent, but as a potential lover, the person you must seduce. Against all other distractions—television, parties, games, his own work—and all those other writers, you must succeed in making your reader wish to embrace you first.

In my notebooks over the years I have listed many writers' idiosyncrasies and habits, perhaps because these seem to exemplify the struggles we all share. While I cannot always credit the dates or media in which these authors spoke, I can give their parentage, the thing which matters most.

Günter Grass, in an interview, said he works and thinks on his feet; like Hemingway, he even types standing up. Once at work he will write "straight through" a story, doing a complete first draft. He then reads what he has written, and rewrites the whole thing. After this, he says, he "synthesizes the two versions." When this is done, he begins again, rewriting four or five hours a day.

As for his personal life, Grass said he takes time for a very large breakfast, skips lunch, and "in the evening I cook for my five children!" Many writing women will empathize with this.

On the other hand, Edward Albee, like Marquand more deliberate in his habits, says his writing depends on a "great deal of rumination, most of it unconscious." This is done in advance of actual writing, so that once Albee is at his typewriter he knows precisely where he is going. He too makes a first draft, which he corrects in pencil; then a second draft, after which his work "is close to its final shape."

Norman Mailer speaks of having written without knowing where the work was going from day to day. And he refers to the energy that comes from work itself. "I always felt as if I were not writing the story myself, but rather as if I were serving as a subject for some intelligence which had decided to use me to write the book." Or short story. Or play. Or any work that a writer may imagine, and bring to pass.

Hemingway has written: "I always worked until I had something done, and I always stopped when I knew what was going to happen next. That way I could be sure of going on the next day."

There have been certain stimuli which I have found helpful for work.

First, and always, one should read, recognize, and dwell on the form itself. It is not enough simply to read what comes along; it is necessary to keep thinking and seeing and shaping characters and ideas and events as writers over the years have shaped them *into the short story form.* That is to say, we should see life in its fictional reality with our reading of the masters—Anton Chekhov, Henry James, D. H. Lawrence, Bernard Malamud, and the others who have held us captive for the times we have devoted to them. We must not see life in the form of slogans or recorded facts, or political tracts, right or left, but as art as we understand it. Mailer and Truman Capote can take journalistic subjects and give them some of the extra dimensions of fiction, but they know what they are doing; the rest of us had better let "real" characters simply provide a springboard for our imaginations in fiction.

Early on in life, it is likely one has discovered that one is, or is not, primarily a word person, one who tastes, and savors, and examines words at least with as much excitement as one responds to music, or painting, or even social intercourse—although each art helps nourish a writer's talent, and each discipline enriches another. Still, primarily writers are readers, but a word of warning here. *It is necessary to write as much as you read,* lest you become an academician or a critic, and lose the sense of abandon that is also a part of the fiction writer's anima.

Above all, respect and cultivate a fever for writing and give in to the passion for work once you have started; once your fiction juices are flowing freely you must, as in a love affair, feel the passion, or the effort is not worth your time.

Of course almost any emotion may stimulate the urge to write: love, pain, a sense of injustice, hatred, even jealousy.

Even boredom is an emotion, which can lead us into taking steps perhaps into anger, or generosity, or contempt, forcing us to abandon preoccupation with ourselves alone, seeking out other lives whose stories, as they connect with our imagination, will release us dramatically from our ennui. Know that for the duration we must henceforth live with them, perform outside ourselves, which is what escape fiction to the reader or writer is all about—but that is only one degree of our involvement. By focusing on a truer vision, searching far beyond the obvious into that stage where work becomes a form of play, we will achieve a state of satisfaction which successfully practicing writers share. Where everything is colored by our obsession and there is a fine feeling which comes from putting the right words on a page, as in having said words to a loved one which further strengthen and advance an intimate and important relationship.

We may even become conscious of our heartbeats as our imagination rises, driving us along unresisting into the unknown, recording, yes, the wart on the side of the loved one's nose, the limp in the dancing foot, the imperfections in a lover's voice; but we concentrate always on the important thing, the story. Time enough later in the finishing stages to settle down to less impulsive considerations of our work, to correcting any misunderstandings or awkwardness our passion may have led us into.

William Faulkner once said in an interview that he considered writing to be "99 percent talent, 99 percent discipline, and 99 percent work." The writer must never be satisfied with what he does. "It never is as good as it can be done," he said. "Always dream and shoot higher than you know you can do. Don't bother just to be better than your contemporaries or predecessors. Try to be better than yourself."

Which just about sums up all that has been said in this chapter. Except for one thing.

Whit once remarked that a lot of people think it would be awfully pleasant to be an author, if only you didn't have to work at it.

6

The Stages of a Story: Beginning

"IF YOU can't catch the reader's attention at the start and hold it, there's no use going on," said the poet Marianne Moore. Marianne was a very wise woman with the innocent face of a mischievous child, the style of a Victorian lady, the wit of a French courtesan, and the energy of a lumberjack. Perhaps her most famous line, which has not always been accredited to her, will remain, "If you've got it, flaunt it!"

More cautiously she admitted, "I am very careful with my first lines. . . . I put it down. I scrutinize it. I test it. I evaluate it." For any poet or short story writer understands it is from these first lines that the work of the writer's imagination will spring, or flow into the task of creation to follow.

The initial problem is to attract, even to compel, the reader's attention, and to hold it as you go on into your story. Obviously a strong opening is essential. Observe, for example, the trained singer's method of attacking her song, how she strikes the opening notes with full breath and vocal authority, instantly compelling her listeners' participation. So too the writer. A weak beginning in a story is as ineffective as breathy and faltering notes by an inexperienced singer in her song.

The discipline and practice of one art can lead to better understanding of another. Isadora Duncan, who created her own original and unique dances, wrote in her autobiography that for her the creative impulse manifested itself first in the region of the solar plexus! When she felt a stirring and excitement in that part of her body, she knew the moment to release the actual dance was upon her. So too will a writer feel the impact of a story he wishes to write, with anticipation, and a stirring in his guts.

Let us go to a painter for advice on beginning work. Robert Henri, when faced with a new and unmarked canvas, cautions: "Be blind to what is not relative." For the writer this means do not begin with useless descriptions, indirect focus, flowery language, and characters or clues which have nothing to do with the story you would tell. Henri also advises us to keep in mind "the larger masses between which you will want to establish harmonies and contrasts." Later on, you will fill your canvas with "light, shade, and details," but at the beginning keep your words uncluttered. Translated for the writer, this means adding all the metaphors, subtleties, complexities, characters, and descriptions your story can stand, *after your basic story is down on paper.*

Said another way, we have Chekhov's often quoted warning to story writers, that it is "in our openings we are most likely to lie." Also, it is in our first sentences and paragraphs that we have what may be our only chance to catch a reader's attention and convince him we have something to say before he is caught up by something, or someone, else.

At this point, let us also be warned that the writer had better not first tell his story verbally before settling down at his typewriter. Unfortunately, when one does this, too often the actual writing is never done. I know of only one case where telling first worked out well. Ludwig Bemelmans, who came from Bavaria to study the American hotel business, was a great raconteur. He delighted friends with witty and entertaining tales about characters he had known in his Prussian, pre-Hitler days in European hotels, and finally Whit Burnett prevailed on him to write these out in short story form. Published, and brought further to life with his irreverent illustrations, Bemelmans's work is now among collectors' treasures today.

One more cautionary note before you begin: never write a story that has been told you by someone else. It may seem new and original when you hear it, but too often it is not. Very young writers, eager for recognition, have been known to copy stories told or read by another, innocently or not, and the resulting charge of plagiarism is hard for both student and sponsor to bear.

And it's not only the young who are guilty. We once found that a story we were on the verge of printing was copied with few changes from a Bemelmans story of some years past—by a California chief of police!

Of course no story can be completely original, since human nature provides the same basic plots year after year. And when a writer is unable to resist putting down on paper a story in his own terms, and if his style and point of view are most markedly his own, the result still can seem to be unique.

An oft-told tale we published some years after the end of World War II was sent us "over the transom," as the saying goes, at a time when tourists were once again beginning to discover Europe in peacetime.

The story began this way:

"Denise and John had been married about a year when they suddenly decided to go to France. Many of the things they did together in London were compounded on the spur of the moment. They were that sort of people. Sometimes they just didn't bother to think things through."

They also take a mother-in-law along and make a quick sortie into Spain.

It is on the way back that they discover why the mother has been uncharacteristically silent: she is dead, apparently a natural death.

57

Distressed, and traveling in a strange country, not knowing the laws or the manner of reporting a death, the young couple decide to drive on, successfully getting through the Spanish border formalities by explaining that the mother is asleep in the back seat.

Finally, after driving many miles, in exhaustion they stop for a brief rest and refreshment at a roadside inn. Relaxing for the first time, they stay longer than they'd expected. When they return they find the car is gone, apparently stolen from the side of the road where they had parked it, with the dead mother's body in it.

Although this chapter of the book is primarily about the beginning of your stories, so logically was this one developed and so well prepared for the ending were we by the first-paragraph description of the young couple's character, it seems only fair to go on to the conclusion.

Hastily, Denise and John telephone their solicitor in London, who advises them to come home at once; but because they so well concealed the facts of the death, and the car's theft, they are never able to collect from the mother's sizable estate; nor is the car, or the woman, ever heard of again.

That story provided the kind of note editors like now and then— a story not too serious, but suspenseful, well written, and apparently original. However, on publication, letters came in and many persons met at cocktail parties had the same tale to tell, in variations. Somewhere such a thing had occurred, but who could actually claim it as his own?

Jorge Luis Borges, the Argentinian poet and writer of stories, once told a gathering of writers that he "senses" a plot from the very moment he begins to write. While E. M. Forster maintained that "plot" and "story" are two different things, Borges sees them as interdependent; only when he is sure of his "plot" from beginning to end can he be sure he has his "story."

He also said, however, "When I first started writing, I used the wrong method. I wrote paragraph by paragraph, changing as I went along. Now, I have found the right method: write as much as I can, first, and then go back and rewrite."

Of course, the methods of no two writers are alike, as has been said before. Each approaches a story in his own way, from his own memory and habits and understanding.

I myself will first try out opening sentences, and attack, in my mind before writing anything on paper. For me there is no substitute for this preliminary mental gathering together of essential elements, even in sentence form, before committing myself to the story. Unfortunately, 3 A.M. is my most productive time, and—while often enough I may not be able to remember my words precisely by morning—somehow between sleep again and waking, my subconscious will have focused on my subject, established the mood I wish to evoke, and whetted my appetite to get on with the game. I can hope that in the morning the blank page in my typewriter will seem cooperative rather than antagonistic.

Once you have made a decision to write, and set the stage for work without interruption, from here on every sentence must carry a conviction of logic and inevitability. A story is, according to dictionary definition, "A narrative, usually of fictitious events, intended to entertain a reader."

If we add to that "plot: a secret plan to accomplish some questionable purpose; a conspiracy," we can stop dreaming and get under way.

Now, having begun your story—the opening sentences, a clear focus on the general direction of your story, and the characters—there is only one method of work that will eventually enable you to reach your goal. *You simply put one foot before the other, without thinking self-consciously along the way.* Let us say you have your azimuth, your lode star to guide you, but little else. And this is as it should be. It cannot be emphasized too often that at least the appearance of spontaneity, if not the actual existence of ingenuousness, is an element to be desired in all the arts (with the possible exception of music). Art *is* an expression of feeling, and where the feeling is, there should be no suspicion of coldly calculated actions or effects. We may say a woman is a "natural flirt" and forgive her; but if we use the opposite if somewhat outmoded term "gold-digger," our response changes. And a Jackson Pollock canvas is worth thousands more than a technically perfect illustration for soap.

To examine some effective openings, let's look at the following:

Katherine Anne Porter, beginning "The Leaning Tower": "Early one morning on his sixth day in Berlin, on the twenty-seventh of December, 1931, Charles Upton left his dull little hotel in Hedemaus-trasse and escaped to the café across the street."

This is a perfect opening for a story about a shy and romantic young Texan who has for years dreamed of going to Berlin, and who eventually becomes depressed and disillusioned, even frightened, by what he finds in the early Hitler days.

Carson McCullers's story "The Jockey" opens: "The jockey came to the doorway of the dining room, then after a moment stepped to one side and stood motionless, with his back to the wall." This story of a jockey cracking up because of an accident to his buddy is little more than a sketch, but the first sentence belongs to the whole and no words are wasted.

Then we may read D. H. Lawrence, whose short stories nearly always open with clear and explicit information and images, but race on into psychological depths beyond any the reader may have anticipated. For example, "Two Blue Birds" begins:

> There was a woman who loved her husband, but she could not live with him. The husband on his side was sincerely attached to his wife, yet he could not live with her. They were both under forty, both handsome and both attractive. They had the most sincere regard for one another, and felt, in some odd way, eternally married to one another. They knew one another more intimately than they knew anybody else, they felt more known to one another than to any other person. Yet they could not live together.

And so we read on into a story of a triangle—the husband, his wife, and the mouselike secretary who wins out in the end.

Mark Twain in "Buck Fanshaw's Funeral" starts with his usual wit: "Someone has said that in order to know a community, one must observe the style of its funerals and know what manner of men they bury with the most ceremony." Seems that Buck Fanshaw kept a "sumptuous" saloon, with a dashing helpmate whom he could have discarded without the formality of a divorce. He had held a high position in the fire department. And so on. But the reader knows the story is about more than that, and keeps on to learn how Buck's friend Scotty Briggs persuades a "parson" to give Buck a fancy burial by converting him first.

Then Milan Kundera: "There had been a time when Marketa disliked her mother-in-law." The title "Mother," ironic juxtaposition with that first line, prepares us for a shrewish woman; a dilemma—what is Marketa going to do about it?—and so leads us into a story of family relations from this provocative beginning: but the mother-in-law makes her own decision to leave because she has *her* own life to lead.

Each of these authors obviously knows where he is going, and uses the opening lines so effectively we feel we may with confidence go through any complexities necessary to follow his story.

Finally, we have Ray Bradbury again. Once you have decided on your own beginning, he says, simply, "Don't think about it. Just do. Think afterward!"

It's not all that simple of course, but if the basis of the story has taken root in your imagination, if you have a compelling reason to write about events around characters and find drama and wit in the bargain, you will have no problem with your beginning. But remember—sharpen your pencil and your wits, don't forget that less can be more, and attack your opening with as much breath and determination as the singer on a stage.

"Everybody who has any respect for painting," says Robert Henri, "feels scared when he starts a new canvas!"

61

7

The Stages of a Story: Continuing to the End

OF ALL THE virtues a writer may cultivate, one that is not usually stressed, but should be, is the ability to get on with the story and finish what has been started in the first flush of inspiration. Hundreds of stories never get beyond page two. Some never get beyond the title. The richness of material may be there, the theme and meaning, the characters ready for their second life. You have told yourself something of what your story is to be about; you have the dominant character, or characters, and your opening lines; you are even anticipating, perhaps not verbally but in some deeper recess of your imagination, the stage at which your crisis, or explosion, is called for. So, unless author persistence is lacking, you now have the rumblings of an unwritten story and a start on paper.

You also will have determined your point of view, the pace and timing of your action or plot, and the setting in which this action must take place. Above all, your story will be pointed in a certain direction, and you, the author, will have some idea of the time it will take to reach your point of no return: the approximate length of the journey. A short story may be as short as a few hundred words, or as long as six or seven thousand words.

At this point you plunge ahead, keeping your eyes on general signs of direction but never for an instant losing sight of the development, the essential point of drama in your story. You will muster all your efforts, gifts, and inventiveness in order to keep your hypothetical reader riding along with you until you have reached your destination. And the only assurance you have that he will want to be with you to the end—since any reader is after all still an unknown quantity —is that you are totally concerned with keeping him there and are deeply committed to not losing your way.

Here we cannot stress too often that *your own credibility to a reader is equal only to the quality of belief you yourself are putting into the venture.* Helping this credibility along and skillfully maintaining the logic and tension in your story are best achieved by never quite losing the question you have raised in the reader's mind: what will happen next?

It is in pursuit of the answer that our drama develops, that the story will rise and fall from its own interior power. In a short story this may happen in three basic ways: at the beginning, with the gun going off at dawn and seeming to shatter the universe; in the middle, with the rise of intensity, and then a more ordered conclusion; or in an old-fashioned way, with a bang-up conclusion coming at us at the end.

The first method of telling your story, starting with chaos and gradually working on to some final acceptance or solution in the lives of your characters, is demonstrated in John Updike's "Domestic Life in America." Fraser, at the very opening, is faced with the crisis of divorce, but when he pays a visit to his wife and children he is drawn back temporarily into the familiar domestic routine and warmth, and the reader's attention shifts. But he then returns to his mistress, whom he plans to marry, until other tensions begin to rise: she complains, and her young son suddenly rejects the situation and telephones his own father to come and take him away. The planned solution of Fraser's life situation as a result of the divorce is again in doubt.

After several minor crises, each inconclusive, Fraser goes back once more to his own children and his not-yet-divorced wife, who asks him to stay; but, logically, he leaves again for the neutral ground of his own apartment, "his room-and-a-half, his askew rug and unmade bed, its dirty windows, and beckoning warmth." The explosive situation in Fraser's marital life at the beginning is relentlessly dissipated into solitude at the end of this cleverly crafted story.

Another story may begin with calm and existing order, proceed with rising intensity to an explosion at the center, and work back down to a final but different order at the end which, of course, can never be quite the same as the beginning. In my story "Eighteenth Summer," mentioned earlier, the beginning is the existing order of the young people's lives, until an alien element, the new girl, is brought in, and the resulting chaos breaks up their compact circle of friendship and trust. But the pieces begin to come together again when Jean leaves the crowd and rows her younger brother, who has had too much to drink, back across the lake toward home. From looking through collected magazines over the years and books of stories, it would seem that the middle-rise story is now predominant, with irony more often than not the final word on the dramatic action. No more *deus ex machina* in which an explosion from outside hastens the denouement, as in some stories by earlier generations of writers, certainly the more popular ones.

And yet in *STORY* we published some marvelously effective tales in which the interest—or chase, or direction, or climax—rises so effectively toward the end that the story's weight is balanced well enough for the reader to accept the final conclusion. Among such stories, one which I particularly liked was "The Siege of Brooklyn Bridge," by Richard Walton.

Harry Nelson, who has not been to war, used to "listen to the vets tell their war stories . . . he was jealous." Living with his wife Mary "just the kind of life she had always wanted," he saw no chance that he could ever chuck it all and go out looking for adventure. Still he "tried to convince himself that someday, something would happen."

It was on a lunchtime away from his office when he was taking a long restless walk that he caught sight of Brooklyn Bridge with its immense Gothic pylons and huge suspension cables "like delicate strands at that distance, arching gracefully across the East River," and he knew what he must do. From that point on Harry began planning how he would climb the Brooklyn Bridge "just as a climber would plan the assault on a mountain, or a soldier, a battle."

The author here accurately specifies the length of the bridge, the number of suspension cables "each about 16 inches in diameter, rising at a 30-degree angle up to the tops of the pink granite pylons." Harry sees that it will be necessary to cross the thirty-foot roadways on a girder in order to reach the outer cable, although barbed-wire barriers have been erected across each cable "to prevent just such adventures as the one he planned."

Day after day Harry plans, surprised that in the excitement he feels no fear. And when the target date arrives, he kisses Mary good-bye, telling her he is going on a business trip. Instead he indulges himself by checking into the Plaza Hotel, taking a hansom ride in Central Park, and eating a hamburger at P. J. Clarke's; finally, at 2 A.M., he writes a note to Mary and sets out for the bridge.

"He found, even though his heart was pounding, that he was still calm. The East River was a sleek black mirror streaked with light."

From here on, we read the breathtaking account of Harry's attempt to cross the bridge by its cables. When he is 175 feet above the water he is still only a quarter of the way to the top.

Now, he begins asking himself what he is doing it all for, thinking that if only he were back home in bed with Mary, how safe he would be. The wind gets stronger, then a hard rain comes down with lightning "hurling itself at Manhattan's towers and thunder crashing around him."

But the storm ends, and the night is beautiful. He can see warships tied up in the Brooklyn Navy Yard, and Manhattan is "ablaze with a million lights." And so he keeps on climbing.

Next, after steadily increasing dangers hundreds of feet above the

East River, where the lifelines are loose and slippery with water, he is hanging from a projection on top of the pylon. With aching fingers, he tries to pull himself up, and fails. After teetering precariously, he falls, landing heavily on the suspension cable.

Then "with one last desperate act he grabbed a cable with both hands. It shuddered and his arms felt torn from their sockets, as he hung there 200 feet above the black water."

But he lowers himself to an intersecting vertical cable, then works his way down to the next cable, where he keeps moving until he reaches the roadway. There, struggling to his feet he limps off the bridge, his clothes torn and his whole body throbbing with pain.

But he was alive. "Christ! He was alive!"

The last line is masterful. But before he did anything—"Before he went home to Mary, or found a bar, or went to his office, he decided to sit down for a while and watch the sun come up over his bridge." *His* bridge!

This is a story which could have begun almost from a random thought—what sort of person would have such a reckless idea, and what would he do about it, and how would it end? A question is asked, and a story answers it. The idea becomes an acceptable short story as the writer keeps driving through to the end, letting the whole thing happen as in an actual experience—or so we can believe.

And this is how a story, well begun, may be concluded.

Whatever your means of getting on with your story, there is one thing of which you may be sure: by simply putting down one foot in front of another you will not only keep your story in motion, you will find that the story helps to write itself. Buried experiences and the little-known subconscious will somehow combine and all sorts of improvisations will offer themselves to you once the idea has taken hold in the initial stages. While you will reject some, others will open doors to insights and possibilities perhaps not even glimpsed in the beginning. (I have said this before in different ways, but it bears repeating. One's instincts must be trusted!)

But sometimes something happens. Sometimes we come to a sudden stop, as though we'd reached a point where our enthusiasm, for no discernible reason, seems to have abandoned us. Where the forward drive once generated so forcefully seems blocked, like an engine run out of fuel. Here we may turn from our typewriters and curse the darkness—but sometimes after a day or so the drive returns and we finish our trip.

Unfortunately, it does not always happen this way. Sometimes the block over one piece of work seems to become permanent; all our writing is throttled, stopped, unable to go on, and panic sets in. I have experienced this; most writers have at one time or another. Sometimes it even comes after a particularly pleasant success; sometimes after a long period of inactivity in writing due to external causes; sometimes from simple fatigue. And sometimes from more serious causes. Whatever the causes, this, which seems at first merely an interruption, can (and often does) become the Writer's Block.

When panic grips us, at times only an analyst can put us straight, maybe by revealing something in our writing our mother would have punished us for, or by uncovering a feeling of guilt because in the pleasures of writing we are neglecting something else we think we should be doing. Only an analyst can supply the answer, perhaps. Then, sometimes when the block has been lifted we find new strengths and produce stories more vigorously than before.

For my part, I have had only temporary blocks, and I think this is because of a method I discovered for myself long ago, simpleminded as it does seem. I try not to panic; I do not force a thing. Instead I take a break, with a drink or some food, or indulge in some trivial conversation with a friend. I may even take a nap. Then, when such frivolity is ended, I sit back at my typewriter and ignore where I left off, instead plunging into the very *end* of my story.

This I write with full concentration, until gradually I creep back and fill in as one may, in relating an episode to an audience, go back and recall matters left out in the first telling. By this time panic has

67

disappeared, and often enough the story turns out better than the original conception.

Seán O'Faoláin makes an analogy not so different from this. He says the writer is the eye discovering the object like a camera starting to move from one angle to another, withdrawing to a distance to enclose a larger view, slipping deftly from one character to another, all the while holding firm in the planned direction. In the story we are writing, skipping about a bit will eventually return us to the basic reason for selecting, in the first place, the development that has been troubling us.

8

The Final Stages

Now, here in ten, twenty, thirty pages is your story, which may be in its final form a masterpiece or, regrettably, may be stillborn and never be seen in the light of any reader's scrutiny. But don't let that bother you; if you have written one story, you may write a thousand, and if you keep working at your skills, *some* will be masterpieces. Don't, whatever you do, cling to one story for years on end like a devoted mother with an only child. Instead, get on with another.

You may, as Ray Bradbury says he did in his twenties, write one story a week, after charting each intervening day as follows: Monday, he wrote the first draft; Tuesday the second; Wednesday the third; Thursday the fourth; and Friday the fifth and final version. Then on Saturday at noon he sent away the story to an editor. On Sunday he started to dream up a new one.

Most writers, however, do put a story away after the first draft, and come back to it later. And sometimes it is better, after the final draft, to still wait a bit until you can read it through with a totally impartial eye that comes after some removal. It has been my own experience that one is seldom able to judge one's own work successfully when it is new and still raw from the pains of birth or glossed with the author's euphoria at having given birth, perhaps the most ephemeral stage of all. Therefore, it is usually advisable, even essential, to abandon your newborn for forty-eight hours, or for one hundred and forty-eight hours, as though it were a changeling you are not yet sure you wish to claim. Put it aside and do not trifle with it at this time. Neither embellish nor edit your story until it has had a chance to breathe better, when your own mind and the strength of your critical judgment will have been renewed.

Schizophrenic behavior? It can't be helped. Certainly at least two minds are required of any fiction writer: the plunger and un-self-conscious doer; and the critic. Your success as a writer will likely lie in separating the two in the exercise of your talents for the good of your story.

In the next stage, the day, the hour, comes when you will sit down and read your story through without a pen in your hand, trying to see it as though written by someone else. You will have left it alone long enough so that, as Sidney Cox wrote, "you will see not what you felt and thought at the time, but what is now on the paper."

It is in the next stage when you read it again that you will expand those passages needing to be amplified and rework those needing to be improved. You will mark your pages freely, crossing out and throwing away with a clear head and a cruel and ruthless disregard, excess verbiage or rhetoric, passages which should be cut, passages which are not *right*. Listen with your ears to the dialogue you have written: read it aloud, attach it clearly to a face, a person, and always try to strip it to the essentials of character, speech patterns, and development of the plot or situation. Write fresh dialogue if the first seems stilted, or put in new dialogue where there was none before. Fill out your descriptions and developments, or condense where you have been profligate; even, perhaps, add new episodes for emphasis and drama.

Then retype entirely (don't ever follow the amateur's way of saving scraps of old typescript and pasting them all together), and read the story again with your first corrections.

Do as Bradbury did, if you find it necessary, rewriting the same story five days of the week! But this is seldom necessary if you allow some time and hold your imagination never too far from your subject. It *is* important to retype more than once and to have the final draft, if you can manage such indulgence, typed by someone else. This removes your story from your own obsession to a reader's judgment in an interesting way: already, another's hands have touched it, another's eyes have followed your logic in a way not even a friendly reader should be trusted with at an early stage. But already you are forced to think in another dimension. Now your story is in a stranger's hands—and will it seem the same when it comes back to you? A typist is not simply a mechanical object, but another pair of eyes and thoughts; perhaps you will want to know what *she* thinks, in a general way. Like a child sent by you to his first day of school, your manuscript is up against something other than your own approval and love: its peers, and other adults.

Finally, *study your story as a whole,* as though you were still another impersonal reader. Ask yourself, Does it hang together in logical development? Are the sequences natural and seemingly inevitable? Are they *right?* Will the ultimate reader—and editor—identify with your characters, or at least be so absorbed by their behavior and thought processes as you have written them that he takes both your story and your authority seriously?

Is your opening—first lines, first paragraphs—provocative and seductive enough so that the reader will be compelled to read on, his own thoughts stimulated by your skill and structural ploys?

Have you made descriptions too elaborate, or have you muffed the physical aspects of your characters or scenes, leaving the reader with no very clear idea of the pictures and images you want him to have?

Are the scenes of action adequate and sufficiently dramatic? Can the entire story be made tighter, more compact, closer to the breathing process of our normal attention span? Have you underwritten, or worse still, overwritten, bringing in descriptions and asides that would be right in a novel but slow the pace in a short story?

Almost half a century ago, Sherwood Anderson wrote his own credo: "The danger lies in the emptiness of so many of the words we use." Each word a fiction writer uses must have meaning, weight, feeling, and particularity.

Finally, to the question "Can writing be taught?"

Yes, if the talent and will are there. Yes, if the teacher or instructor does not impose his own ideas upon the more fragile ones of the students. Yes, if the adviser teaches also the necessity of living and observing and writing and giving and accepting and competing and working and loving. Yes, if this writing is important enough to the writer to make it his major love and maybe more important than anything else he will ever pursue.

And yes, if the instructor stresses the reading of writers old and contemporary, and also of science, poetry, psychology, history, and above all the short fiction made by the masters, as easily available as the nearest television program.

A classroom provides an emphasis on the thing which concerns us most: the short story itself. This focus is something not easily come by in today's living, and a justification for our pursuit of excellence may otherwise be hard to find since there are so many other demanding things most of us could be about.

There is, in a classroom, discussion that is sometimes brutal, not always accurate or helpful, but here we will find fellow craftsmen, who at least take our work seriously. And here beginnings, or mere ideas, for stories will be tossed aside; we must have a finished product to be worthy of the attention of our peers, and this fact in itself has value.

Also, if we are good, we will find evidence that we are good; and if we are not, well, we have seen how others managed to succeed; or we can give it up altogether.

In my own teaching, I gave the usual writing assignments to each class, but with intensive reading in the short story form. This saturation in the form itself is invaluable. Even if the writer later rebels and strikes out in directions for which there is no precedent, at least he knows what he is doing. Salvador Dali, whose iconoclasm and originality startled the world, once told my young stepson that if he would be a painter he must assiduously first study and absorb all the conventional steps and masters: above all he must learn to draw true to life. Not until then could he take chances, try to reeducate the world, impose his own vision upon the art field in which he worked.

9

Selling: Becoming a Professional

"MANY are culled, but few are chosen."

This pun by Whit Burnett actually covers the whole net product of the game. "Culling" is what the first reader at a magazine or publishing house does as he selects from the "slush" pile stories interesting enough to be read at least a second time. The "slush" consists of unsolicited manuscripts; some houses do not accept them at all because there are so many.

Solicited manuscripts, those either requested or discussed in advance with an editor, are something else. The editor will still in most cases have your story read by a trusted first reader, but the fact that it has been brought to an editor's attention will probably cut down on the time taken to come to a decision.

Now. You know enough to have the final version of your story neatly typed in double-space with wide margins and consecutively numbered pages. You will not write "more" at the end of a page, as some newspaper-trained young writers have done, and you will not put a bit of glue between pages midway in your manuscript to test whether or not a busy editor has read it through. (It cannot possibly make you feel any better if on its return you find he has not!)

You will use a manuscript-sized envelope if you prefer not to fold your story, and you will enclose another the same size for its possible return, both adequately stamped and addressed. You will then expect to wait at least two weeks to a month before hearing from the magazine (or a publishing house, for a collection of short stories); then at the end of, say, thirty days, you write a pleasant, humorous (if possible!), and uncomplaining note to the editor inquiring about your manuscript—that is, if your nervous system demands some action! Chances are the editorial staff is behind in its work of reading; or everyone is on vacation; *or* an editor may be seriously considering acceptance of your work. In any case, he will not be in a mood for any author's petulant, complaining, or threatening letter (an author once sent a rope to the editors of *STORY* to hang themselves with), and will return your story with no more ado—a good and literary word in this case.

The process of selection, which of course you do not see, is as follows: When your story is received it will be opened, listed on a file card, and probably acknowledged—most editors do this if possible. It will then be placed among the piles of unsolicited manuscripts to await its turn with that first reader, who may or may not be a regular on the editorial staff. Presumably, however, the first reader is always well read, eager, hardworking, *and* optimistic; and here is where the culling process begins. Stories judged to have interesting possibilities will be sent on to an editor, probably one with limited authority, who is no less eager to find a good story than the first reader; but here, in place of the early optimism is a certain amount of cynicism, which is all to the good. Show me, he says to the story, but I doubt if you can. A reader's strong recommendation to buy your story at this point is important, and this second reading may account for the delay in your hearing the worst, or best.

Now it is up to the senior fiction editor—but not quite. He will make up his mind, but acceptance is rarely certain until there is a meeting of several minds and a discussion as to your story's a) freshness, b) credibility, c) originality, d) suitability for that particular market, e) its possible place in projected editorial plans. Many good stories are "culled but not chosen," but the fault may not lie in the work at hand but in many other factors having nothing to do with the story's worth. Which is not a cheering thought, but a philosophical one you'll have to accept.

But now, okay, your story is accepted, which means you the author will receive a cordial letter of acceptance, noting the price you will be paid and very likely containing some complimentary words on your writing. This is a very pleasant experience for the previously unpublished author, *and* for the one who is "established." For the beginner it means he can now come out of the closet where he has been concealing his writing habits, maybe for years. For the established writer it means he is still a combatant in the field of letters, still able to produce and have his work published. For, believe it or not, there are few among us who do not have rejected manuscripts in our drawers, and a rejection is as painful on a writer's last day as on his first.

All too often, the pursuit of writing will involve economic problems. According to a recent survey by PEN (Poets, Essayists, and Novelists—an organization for already published writers), the first source of income for most of us is in teaching or other related work. Some writers work in publishing houses, some in libraries, or serve as translators, and some spend wearisome, if sometimes stimulating, hours on the lecture circuits. Some are housewives. Nine percent of these professional writers were in the $50,000-a-year bracket; 16 percent were in the $10,000 range; and the rest made $3000 a year or less from writing.

The short story writer whose stories appear in magazines is paid not much more than a writer twenty years ago; no cost-of-living increase in this field! If he is fortunate enough to have a collection of his stories published he, even if he is already a famous "name," may not be better paid until he is awarded a Nobel or a Pulitzer or a National Book Award prize. And sometimes not even then.

A letter written to the editors of *STORY* in the 1940s by Nobel laureate William Faulkner stated: "I have become so damned frantic trying to make a living and keep my grocer, etc., from putting me in bankruptcy for the last year, that nothing I or anybody else ever wrote seems worth anything any more." And yet most of the best fiction writers of our day have written memorable short stories for little more than the unique satisfaction a well-conceived and successfully completed short story can give. Katherine Anne Porter, whose one novel, *Ship of Fools,* made a large sum of money, still is remembered best for her short stories and novellas. Who does not cherish the classic stories of Flannery O'Connor, Eudora Welty, William Saroyan, Bernard Malamud, and John Updike? Yet publishers often hesitate to put out short stories in book form.

"Short stories do not sell!" they will insist, a cliché used by publishers who may not even believe it themselves; in any case it is self-defeating. My own book of stories, many published in magazines here, and abroad in translation, was accepted for publication only because, the editor told me, "we hope to continue publishing your novels, so we'll take a chance on your stories." And the book, *Boarders in the Rue Madame,* was then lost in the trade department, which is where books on dogs, psychoses, cartoons, and cooking are all lumped together!

But this is to digress, or—unfairly perhaps—to discourage writers whose talent in the short story may change the whole picture of publishing. And great stories are being published today, scarce as the markets may be. The important thing, after all, is how we ourselves see our work, how we present our best work to others, and how persistent we are in keeping up the standards that made us fall in love with the perfectibility of the short story in the first place. We will continue to work at this demanding but delightful occupation; we will never cease our constant study of the small dramas acted out of human nature by the human race.

At least let us never be dilettantes, mere scribblers indulging in wishful thinking, desiring the name but not the excitement of doing; let us respect our "trade."

On the other hand, let us not deny the amateur the use of his talents, or even his pride in them. He is still a contributing member of society, we may say, and all right in his place—even though something of a bore to anyone outside his family circle. And some writers remain amateurs forever, proudly proclaiming this the status they prefer, claiming to be "untainted" by professionalism—as though they were athletes in some good-old-boy tradition, caring only to impress other amateurs. Actually, I don't believe them. An amateur writer is either a professional not yet arrived or one who doesn't expect to work hard enough to achieve a goal of excellence and thus merit publication.

Unfortunately those advertisements, "You too can write!" have encouraged countless untalented men and women—mostly women, sad to say—for this promise is within the great American tradition that one may achieve anything one puts one's mind to. "Confidence," that's all one needs to be a great dancer, a great painter, or a great writer. So here we are again at daydreams, but the useless kind.

Once I was teaching an evening extension course at Hunter College in New York when an author-student brought me a story, she proudly announced, that had been criticized by ten other teachers, and she hadn't yet seen the need to change a line. Also it was the only story she had ever written; she would write another when this one *sold.*

I ventured to suggest that with all that advice perhaps she would do better to try again, to write another and different story and submit that for my help and criticism. Unhappily, she stormed out of the class and went straight to the dean, demanding that I be "fired" (her word) since I had no compassion for a talented and sensitive writer.

I suspect from that day to this she is still carrying that one story around from teacher to rejecting editor without ever having changed a word.

Anyhow, serve your apprenticeship, devote as much time as you can to writing, reading, and thinking short stories. Accept advice when it is given but reject criticism when after careful consideration it doesn't seem to fit. Don't be afraid to change, to grow, to experiment, (or to resist), to rewrite—above all, to rewrite, with a passionate devotion to what language can do for you! And never close your mind to subject matter, to new ways of doing or saying things, of writing better and better, or to life itself.

10

The Proof of the Pudding:
Six Stories

WE come now to the final and ultimately most important advice one story writer may give to another who aspires to create sound and enduring works. This first rule is still the easiest and most agreeable to follow: It is simply, *read*.

Go back to the great story writers whose work has not been surpassed, even though the subject matter and style may have the stamp of an earlier time, and analyze why the most memorable of these stories still endure.

Then read your best contemporaries, particularly in the current collections—the O. Henry annual collections, the *Best Short Stories* of the year, the Pushcart Press selections from the "little" magazines, among others—judging them by standards you yourself aspire to. But do not imitate anyone else in your writing any more than you would in expressions of living and loving.

Read; because one could explain endlessly what a short story is and is not, and the results would be the same as if an explorer tried to describe a mirror to a savage who has never looked into one nor seen his own reflection. The short story is our mirror of ourselves, of life as we know it, of human emotions and dilemmas as we have experienced them, and of all the colors we may separate out of the spectrum of the universe. It is our image returned to us as we had not known it could be.

There are stories one remembers, and stories easily forgotten. When we go searching for examples to demonstrate the variety and possibilities and rewards of the form, we find tremendous wealth from which to choose, not only among those cherished through the years, but also today. The quality of magazine fiction is high, even though the quantity has declined, unfortunately, over the past twenty or thirty years. There is still *The New Yorker, Atlantic Monthly, Harper's, Esquire,* many of the large circulation "women's" magazines, and of course those from the college presses, the literary magazines where much of the new talent of today appears. So it was hard to make selections to illustrate this book.

So hard, in fact, that at last I settled on a natural and less difficult solution: to present six stories from the magazine *STORY*, which I co-edited with Whit Burnett for more than thirty years. These are stories which not only interested our readers, subscribers, publishers, and critics, but also found extended life in other media in this country and abroad. Most of these authors have achieved and even surpassed the promise we saw in them then.

ADDRESS UNKNOWN

━━━━━━◆━◇◆◇━◆━━━━━━

Kressmann Taylor

"*ADDRESS UNKNOWN*" *is a story which quickly became a classic in its own time. Written by a husband and wife, Elliot and Kressmann Taylor, it created a sensation when it appeared in* STORY *in 1938. In epistolary form—a form which is frequently abused and almost never to be recommended—the subject, the theme, and the emotion evoked all fall together in a chilling condemnation of the Hitler years in Germany. Since the questions the story asks have never been satisfactorily answered, and since the subject of the Holocaust is still profoundly disturbing, it is a perfect example of how a compelling, well-written story does not date nor stale.*

It may be read still as a modern (and classical) story of friendship and trust and love turned to hatred and finally into an act of revenge as individuals are caught up in the personal and political tragedies of the times. It may also be read as an example of the restraint used by writers to permit a certain kind of story to unfold in logical sequence to its final conclusion without rhetorical explanations or embellishments. The development, and the gradual release of emotion, as when air ever so slowly is released from a balloon, could serve as a model for any story about events which overtake us in periods of swift changes and catastrophes.

Schulse-Eisenstein Galleries
San Francisco, California, U.S.A.
November 12, 1932.

Herrn Martin Schulse
Schloss Rantzenburg
Munich, Germany
My dear Martin:

Back in Germany! How I envy you! Although I have not seen it since my school days, the spell of *Unter den Linden* is still strong upon me—the breadth of intellectual freedom, the discussions, the music, the lighthearted comradeship. And now the old Junker spirit, the Prussian arrogance and militarism are gone. You go to a democratic Germany, a land with a deep culture and the beginnings of a fine political freedom. It will be a good life. Your new address is impressive and I rejoice that the crossing was so pleasant for Elsa and the young sprouts.

As for me, I am not so happy. Sunday morning finds me a lonely bachelor without aim. My Sunday home is now transported over the wide seas. The big old house on the hill—your welcome that said the day was not complete until we were together again! And our dear jolly Elsa, coming out beaming, grasping my hand and shouting "Max, Max!" and hurrying indoors to open my favorite *Schnaps*. The fine boys, too, especially your handsome young Heinrich; he will be a grown man before I set eyes upon him again.

And dinner—shall I evermore hope to eat as I have eaten? Now I go to a restaurant and over my lonely roast beef come visions of *gebackner Schinken* steaming in its Burgundy sauce, of *Spatzle*, ah! of *Spatzle* and *Spargel*! No, I shall never again become reconciled to my American diet. And the wines, so carefully slipped ashore from the German boats, and the pledges we made as the glasses brimmed for the fourth and fifth and sixth times.

Kressmann Taylor

Of course you are right to go. You have never become American despite your success here, and now that the business is so well established you must take your sturdy German boys back to the homeland to be educated. Elsa too has missed her family through the long years and they will be glad to see you as well. The impecunious young artist has now become the family benefactor, and that too will give you a quiet little triumph.

The business continues to go well. Mrs. Levine has bought the small Picasso at our price, for which I congratulate myself, and I have old Mrs. Fleshman playing with the notion of the hideous Madonna. No one ever bothers to tell her that any particular piece of hers is bad, because they are all so bad. However, I lack your fine touch in selling to the old Jewish matrons. I can persuade them of the excellence of the investment, but you alone had the fine spiritual approach to a piece of art that unarmed them. Besides they probably never entirely trust another Jew.

A delightful letter came yesterday from Griselle. She writes that she is about to make me proud of my little sister. She has the lead in a new play in Vienna and the notices are excellent—her discouraging years with the small companies are beginning to bear fruit. Poor child, it has not been easy for her, but she has never complained. She has a fine spirit, as well as beauty, and I hope the talent as well. She asked about you, Martin, in a very friendly way. There is no bitterness left there, for that passes quickly when one is young as she is. A few years and there is only a memory of the hurt, and of course neither of you was to be blamed. Those things are like quick storms, for a moment you are drenched and blasted, and you are so wholly helpless before them. But then the sun comes, and although you have neither quite forgotten, there remains only gentleness and no sorrow. You would not have had it otherwise, nor would I. I have not written Griselle that you are in Europe but perhaps I shall if you think it wise, for she does not make friends easily and I know she would be glad to feel that friends are not far away.

Fourteen years since the war! Did you mark the date? What a long

84

way we have traveled, as peoples, from that bitterness! Again, my dear Martin, let me embrace you in spirit, and with the most affectionate remembrances to Elsa and the boys, believe me,

Your ever most faithful,
Max

Schloss Rantzenburg
Munich, Germany
December 10, 1932.

Mr. Max Eisenstein
Schulse-Eisenstein Galleries
San Francisco, California, U.S.A.
Max, dear old fellow:

The check and accounts came through promptly, for which my thanks. You need not send me such details of the business. You know how I am in accord with your methods, and here at Munich I am in a rush of new activities. We are established, but what a turmoil! The house, as you know, I had long in mind. And I got it at an amazing bargain. Thirty rooms and about ten acres of park; you would never believe it. But then, you could not appreciate how poor is now this sad land of mine. The servants' quarters, stables and outbuildings are most extensive, and would you believe it, we employ now ten servants for the same wages of our two in the San Francisco home.

The tapestries and pieces we shipped make a rich show and some other fine furnishings I have been able to secure, so that we are much admired, I was almost to say envied. Four full services in the finest china I have bought and much crystal, as well as a full service of silver for which Elsa is in ecstasies.

And for Elsa—such a joke! You will, I know, laugh with me. I have purchased for her a huge bed. Such a size as never was before, twice the bigness of a double bed, and with great posters in carved wood. The sheets I must have made to order, for there are no sheets made that could fit it. And they are of linen, the finest linen sheets. Elsa laughs and laughs, and her old *Grossmutter* stands shaking her head and grumbles, "*Nein*, Martin, *nein*. You have made it so and now you must take care or she will grow to match it."

"*Ja*," says Elsa, "five more boys and I will fit it just nice and snug." And she will, Max.

For the boys there are three ponies (little Karl and Wolfgang are not big enough to ride yet) and a tutor. Their German is very bad, being too much mixed with English.

Elsa's family do not find things so easy now. The brothers are in the professions and, while much respected, must live together in one house. To the family we seem American millionaires and while we are far from that yet our American income places us among the wealthy here. The better foods are high in price and there is much political unrest even now under the presidency of Hindenburg, a fine liberal whom I much admire.

Already old acquaintances urge me that I interest myself in administrative matters in the town. This I take under consideration. It may be somewhat to our benefit locally if I become an official.

As for you, my good Max, we have left you alone, but you must not become a misanthrope. Get yourself at once a nice fat little wife who will busy herself with all your cares and feed you into a good humor. That is my advice and it is good, although I smile as I write it.

You write of Griselle. So she wins her success, the lovely one! I rejoice with you, although even now I resent it that she must struggle to win her way, a girl alone. She was made, as any man can see, for luxury and for devotion and the charming and beautiful life where ease allows much play of the sensibilities. A gentle, brave soul is in her dark eyes, but there is something strong as iron and very daring too. She is a woman who does nothing and gives nothing lightly. Alas, dear Max, as always, I betray myself. But although you were silent during our stormy affair, you know that the decision was not easy for me. You never reproached me, your friend, while the little sister suffered, and I have always felt you knew that I suffered too, most gravely. What could I do? There was Elsa and my little sons. No other decision was possible to make. Yet for Griselle I keep a tenderness that will last long after she has taken a much younger man for husband or lover. The old wound has healed but the scar throbs at times, my friend.

I wish that you will give her our address. We are such a short distance from Vienna that she can feel there is for her a home close at hand. Elsa, too, knows nothing of the old feeling between us and you know with what warmth she would welcome your sister, as she would welcome you. Yes, you must tell her that we are here and urge her to soon make a contact with us. Give her our most warm congratulations for the fine success that she is making.

Elsa asks that I send to you her love, and Heinrich would also say "hello" to Uncle Max. We do not forget you, Maxel.

My heartiest greetings to you,

Martin

Schulse-Eisenstein Galleries
San Francisco, California, U.S.A.
January 21, 1933.

Herrn Martin Schulse
Schloss Rantzenburg
Munich, Germany
My dear Martin:

I was glad to forward your address to Griselle. She should have it shortly, if she has not already received it. What jollification there will be when she sees you all! I shall be with you in spirit as heartily as if I also could rejoin you in person.

You speak of the poverty there. Conditions have been bad here this winter, but of course we have known nothing of the privations you see in Germany.

Personally, you and I are lucky that we have such a sound following for the gallery. Of course our own clientele are cutting their purchases but if they buy only half as much as before we shall be comfortable, not extravagantly so, but very comfortable. The oils you sent are excellent, and the prices amazing. I shall dispose of them at an appalling profit almost at once. And the ugly Madonna is gone! Yes, to old Mrs. Fleshman. How I gasped at her perspicacity in recognizing its worth, hesitating to set a price! She suspected me of having another client, and I named an indecent figure. She pounced on it, grinning slyly as she wrote her check. How I exulted as she bore the horror off with her, you alone will know.

Alas, Martin, I often am ashamed of myself for the delight I take in such meaningless little triumphs. You in Germany, with your country house and your affluence displayed before Elsa's relatives, and I in America, gloating because I have tricked a giddy old woman into buying a monstrosity. What a fine climax for two men of forty! Is it for this we spend our lives, to scheme for money and then to strut it publicly? I am always castigating myself, but I continue to do as before. Alas, we are all caught in the same mill. We are vain and we are dishonest because it is necessary to triumph over other vain and dishonest persons. If I do not sell Mrs. Fleshman our horror, somebody else will sell her a worse one. We must accept these necessities.

But there is another realm where we can always find something true, the fireside of a friend, where we shed our little conceits and find warmth and understanding, where small selfishnesses are impossible and where wine and books and talk give a different meaning to existence. There we have made something that no falseness can touch. We are at home.

Who is this Adolf Hitler who seems rising toward power in Germany? I do not like what I read of him.

Embrace all the young fry and our abundant Elsa for

Your ever affectionate,

Max

Schloss Rantzenburg
Munich, Germany
March 25, 1933.

Mr. Max Eisenstein
Schulse-Eisenstein Galleries
San Francisco, California, U.S.A.
Dear old Max:

You have heard of course of the new events in Germany, and you will want to know how it appears to us here on the inside. I tell you truly, Max, I think in many ways Hitler is good for Germany, but I am not sure. He is now the active head of the government. I doubt much that even Hindenburg could now remove him from power, as he was truly forced to place him there. The man is like an electric shock, strong as only a great orator and a zealot can be. But I ask myself, is he quite sane? His brown-shirt troops are of the rabble. They pillage and have started a bad Jew-baiting. But these may be minor things, the little surface scum when a big movement boils up. For I tell you, my friend, there is a surge—a surge. The people everywhere have had a quickening. You feel it in the streets and shops. The old despair has been thrown aside like a forgotten coat. No longer the people wrap themselves in shame; they hope again. Perhaps there may be found an end to this poverty. Something, I do not know what, will happen. A leader is found! Yet cautiously to myself I ask, a leader to where? Despair overthrown often turns us in mad directions.

Publicly, as is natural, I express no doubt. I am now an official and a worker in the new regime and I exult very loud indeed. All of us officials who cherish whole skins are quick to join the National Socialists. That is the name for Herr Hitler's party. But also it is not only expedient, there is something more, a feeling that we of Germany have found our destiny and that the future sweeps toward us in an overwhelming wave. We too must move. We must go with it. Even now there are being wrongs done. The storm troopers are having their moment of victory, and there are bloody heads and sad hearts to show for it. But these things pass; if the end in view is right they pass and are forgotten. History writes a clean new page.

All I now ask myself, and I can say to you what I cannot say to any here is: Is the end right? Do we make for a better goal? For you know, Max, I have seen these people of my race since I came here, and I have learned what agonies they have suffered, what years of less and less bread, of leaner bodies, of the end of hope. The quicksand of despair held them, it was at their chins. Then just before they died a man came and pulled them out. All they now know is, they will not die. They are in hysteria of deliverance, almost they worship him. But whoever the savior was, they would have done the same. God grant it is a true leader and no black angel they follow so joyously. To you alone, Max, I say I do not know. I do not know. Yet I hope.

So much for politics. Ourselves, we delight in our new home and have done much entertaining. Tonight the mayor is our guest, at a 'dinner for twenty-eight. We spread ourselves a little, maybe, but that is to be forgiven. Elsa has a new gown of blue velvet, and is in terror for fear it will not be big enough. She is with child again. There is the way to keep a wife contented, Max. Keep her so busy with babies she has no time to fret.

Our Heinrich has made a social conquest. He goes out on his pony and gets himself thrown off, and who picks him up but the Baron Von Freische. They have a long conversation about America, and one day the baron calls and we have coffee. Heinrich will go there to lunch next week. What a boy! It is too bad his German is not better but he delights everyone.

So we go, my friend, perhaps to become part of great events, perhaps only to pursue our simple family way, but never abandoning that trueness of friendship of which you speak so movingly. Our hearts go out to you across the wide sea, and when the glasses are filled we toast "Uncle Max."

Yours in affectionate regard,

Martin

Schulse-Eisenstein Galleries
San Francisco, California, U.S.A.
May 18, 1933.

Herrn Martin Schulse
Schloss Rantzenburg
Munich, Germany
Dear Martin:

I am in distress at the press reports that come pouring in to us from the Fatherland. Thus it is natural that I turn to you for light while there are only conflicting stories to be had here. I am sure things cannot be as bad as they are pictured. A terrible pogrom, that is the consensus of our American papers.

I know your liberal mind and warm heart will tolerate no viciousness and that from you I can have the truth. Aaron Silberman's son has just returned from Berlin and had, I hear, a narrow escape. The tales he tells of what he has seen, floggings, the forcing of quarts of castor oil through clenched teeth and the consequent hours of dying through the slow agony of bursting guts, are not pretty ones. These things may be true, and they may, as you have said, be but the brutal surface froth of human revolution. Alas, to us Jews they are a sad story familiar through centuries of repetition, and it is almost unbelievable that the old martyrdom must be endured in a civilized nation today. Write me, my friend, and set my mind at ease.

Griselle's play will come to a close about the end of June after a great success. She writes that she has an offer for another role in Vienna and also for a very fine one in Berlin for the autumn. She is talking most of the latter one, but I have written her to wait until the anti-Jewish feeling has abated. Of course she uses another name which is not Jewish (Eisenstein would be impossible for the stage anyway), but it is not her name that would betray her origin. Her features, her gestures, her emotional voice proclaim her a Jewess no matter what she calls herself, and if this feeling has any real strength she had best not venture into Germany just at present.

Forgive me, my friend, for so distrait and brief a letter but I cannot rest until you have reassured me. You will, I know, write in all fairness. Pray do so at once.

With the warmest protestations of faith and friendship for you and yours, I am ever your faithful

Max

Deutsch-Voelkische Bank und
Handelsgesellschaft, München
July 9, 1933.

Mr. Max Eisenstein
Schulse-Eisenstein Galleries
San Francisco, California, U.S.A.
Dear Max:

You will see that I write upon the stationery of my bank. This is necessary because I have a request to make of you and I wish to avoid the new censorship which is most strict. We must for the present discontinue writing each other. It is impossible for me to be in correspondence with a Jew even if it were not that I have an official position to maintain. If a communication becomes necessary you must enclose it with the bank draft and not write to me at my house again.

As for the stern measures that so distress you, I myself did not like them at first, but I have come to see their painful necessity. The Jewish race is a sore spot to any nation that harbors it. I have never hated the individual Jew—yourself I have always cherished as a friend, but you will know that I speak in all honesty when I say I have loved you, not because of your race but in spite of it.

The Jew is the universal scapegoat. This does not happen without reason, and it is not the old superstition about "Christ-killers" that makes them distrusted. But this Jew trouble is only an incident. Something bigger is happening.

If I could show you, if I could make you see—the rebirth of this new Germany under our Gentle Leader! Not for always can the world grind a great people down in subjugation. In defeat for fourteen years we bowed our heads. We ate the bitter bread of shame and drank the thin gruel of poverty. But now we are free men. We rise in our might and hold our heads up before the nations. We purge our bloodstream of its baser elements. We go singing through our valleys with strong muscles tingling for a new work—and from the mountains ring the voices of Wotan and Thor, the old, strong gods of the German race.

But no. I am sure as I write, as with the new vision my own enthusiasm burns, that you will not see how necessary is all this for Germany. You will see only that your own people are troubled. You will not see that a few must suffer for the millions to be saved. You will be a Jew first and wail for your people. This I understand. It is the Semitic character. You lament but you are never brave enough to fight back. That is why there are pogroms.

Alas, Max, this will pain you, I know, but you must realize the truth. There are movements far bigger than the men who make them up. As for me, I am a part of the movement. Heinrich is an officer in the boys' corp which is headed by Baron Von Freische whose rank is now shedding a luster upon our house, for he comes often to visit with Heinrich and Elsa, whom he much admires. Myself, I am up to the ears in work. Elsa concerns herself little with politics except to adore our Gentle Leader. She gets tired too easily this last month. Perhaps the babies come too fast. It will be better for her when this one is born.

I regret our correspondence must close this way, Max. Perhaps we can someday meet again on a field of better understanding.

As ever, your
Martin Schulse

San Francisco
August 1, 1933.

Herrn Martin Schulse
(kindness of J. Lederer)
Schloss Rantzenburg
Munich, Germany
Martin, my old friend:

I am sending this by the hand of Jimmy Lederer, who will shortly pass through Munich on a European vacation. I cannot rest after the letter you last sent me. It is so unlike you I can only attribute its contents to your fear of the censorship. The man I have loved as a brother, whose heart has ever been brimming with sympathy and friendship, cannot possibly partake of even a passive partnership in the butchery of innocent people. I trust and pray that it may be so, that you will write me no exposition, which might be dangerous for you,—only a simple "yes." That will tell me that you play the part of expediency but that your heart has not changed, and that I was not deluded in believing you to be always a man of fine and liberal spirit to whom wrongs are wrongs in whosoever's name they may be committed.

This censorship, this persecution of all men of liberal thought, the burning of libraries and corruption of the universities would arouse your antagonism if there had been no finger laid on one of my race in Germany. You are a liberal, Martin. You have always taken the long view. I know that you cannot be swept away from sanity by a popular movement which has so much that is bad about it, no matter how strong it may be.

I can see why the Germans acclaim Hitler. They react against the very real wrongs which have been laid on them since the disaster of the war. But you, Martin, have been almost an American since the war. I know that it is not my friend who has written to me, that it will prove to have been only the voice of caution and expediency.

Eagerly I await the one word that will set my heart at peace. Write your "yes" quickly.

My love to you all,

Max

Deutsch-Voelkische Bank und
Handelsgesellschaft, München
August 18, 1933.

Mr. Max Eisenstein
Schulse-Eisenstein Galleries
San Francisco, California, U.S.A.
Dear Max:

I have your letter. The word is "no." You are a sentimentalist. You do not know that all men are not cut to your pattern. You put nice little tags on them, like "liberal" and expect them to act so-and-so. But you are wrong. So, I am an American liberal? No! I am a German patriot.

A liberal is a man who does not believe in doing anything. He is a talker about the rights of man, but just a talker. He likes to make a big noise about freedom of speech, and what is freedom of speech? Just the chance to sit firmly on the backside and say that whatever is being done by the active men is wrong. What is so futile as the liberal? I know him well because I have been one. He condemns the passive government because it makes no change. But let a powerful man arise, let an active man start to make a change, then where is your liberal? He is against it. To the liberal any change is the wrong one.

He calls this the "long view," but it is merely a bad scare that he will have to do something himself. He loves words and high-sounding precepts but he is useless to the men who make the world what it is. These are the only important men, the doers. And here in Germany a doer has risen. A vital man is changing things. The whole tide of a people's life changes in a minute because the man of action has come. And I join him. I am not just swept along by a current. The useless life that was all talk and no accomplishment I drop. I put my back and shoulders behind the great new movement. I am a man because I act. Before that I am just a voice. I do not question the ends of our action. It is not necessary. I know it is good because it is so vital. Men are not drawn into bad things with so much joy and eagerness.

You say we persecute men of liberal thought, we destroy libraries. You should wake from your musty sentimentalizing. Does the surgeon spare the cancer because he must cut to remove it? We are cruel. Of course we are cruel. As all birth is brutal, so is this new birth of ours. But we rejoice. Germany lifts high her head among the nations of the world. She follows her glorious Leader to triumph. What can you know of this, you who only sit and dream? You have never known a Hitler. He is a drawn sword. He is a white light, but hot as the sun of a new day.

I must insist that you write no further. We are no longer in sympathy, as now we must both realize.

Martin Schulse

Eisenstein Galleries
San Francisco, California, U.S.A.
September 5, 1933.

Herrn Martin Schulse
c/o Deutsch-Voelkische Bank
und Handelsgesellschaft
Munich, Germany
Dear Martin:

Enclosed are your draft and the month's accounts. It is of necessity that I send a brief message. Griselle has gone to Berlin. She is too daring. But she has waited so long for success she will not relinquish it, and laughs at my fears. She will be at the Koenig Theater. You are an official. For old friendship's sake, I beg of you to watch over her. Go to Berlin if you can and see whether she is in danger.

It will distress you to observe that I have been obliged to remove your name from the firm's name. You know who our principal clients are, and they will touch nothing now from a firm with a German name.

Your new attitude I cannot discuss. But you must understand me. I did not expect you would take up arms for my people because they are my people, but because you were a man who loved justice.

I commend my rash Griselle to you. The child does not realize what a risk she is taking, I shall not write again.

Goodbye, my friend,

Max

Eisenstein Galleries
San Francisco, California, U.S.A.
November 5, 1933.

Herrn Martin Schulse
c/o Deutsch-Voelkische Bank
und Handelsgesellschaft
Munich, Germany
Martin:

I write again because I must. A black foreboding has taken possession of me. I wrote Griselle as soon as I knew she was in Berlin and she answered briefly. Rehearsals were going brilliantly; the play would open shortly. My second letter was more encouragement than warning, and it has been returned to me, the envelope unopened, marked only addressee unknown (*Adressat Unbekannt*). What a darkness those words carry! How can she be unknown? It is surely a message that she has come to harm. They know what has happened to her, those stamped letters say, but I am not to know. She has gone into some sort of void and it will be useless to seek her. All this they tell me in two words, *Adressat Unbekannt*.

Martin, need I ask you to find her, to succor her? You have known her graciousness, her beauty and sweetness. You have had her love, which she has given to no other man. Do not attempt to write to me. I know I need not even ask you to aid. It is enough to tell you that something has gone wrong, that she must be in danger.

I leave her in your hands, for I am helpless.

Max

Eisenstein Galleries
San Francisco, California, U.S.A.
November 23, 1933.

Herrn Martin Schulse
c/o Deutsch-Voelkische Bank
und Handelsgesellschaft
Munich, Germany
Martin:

I turn to you in despair. I could not wait for another month to pass so I am sending some information as to your investments. You may wish to make some changes and I can thus enclose my appeal with a bank letter.

It is Griselle. For two months there has been only silence from her, and now the rumors begin to come in to me. From Jewish mouth to Jewish mouth the tales slowly come back from Germany, tales so full of dread I would close my ears if I dared, but I cannot. I must know what has happened to her. I must be sure.

She appeared in the Berlin play for a week. Then she was jeered from the audience as a Jewess. She is so headstrong, so foolhardy, the splendid child! She threw the word back in their teeth. She told them proudly that she *was* a Jewess.

Some of the audience started after her. She ran backstage. Someone must have helped her for she got away with the whole pack at her heels and took refuge with a Jewish family in a cellar for several days. After that she changed her appearance as much as she could and started south, hoping to walk back to Vienna. She did not dare try the railroads. She told those she left that she would be safe if she could reach friends in Munich. That is my hope, that she has gone to you, for she has never reached Vienna. Send me word, Martin, and if she has not come there make a quiet investigation if you can. My mind cannot rest. I torture myself by day and by night, seeing the brave little thing trudging all those long miles through hostile country,

99

with winter coming on. God grant you can send me a word of relief.

Max

Deutsch-Voelkische Bank und
Handelsgesellschaft, München
December 8, 1933.

Heil Hitler! I much regret that I have bad news for you. Your sister is dead. Unfortunately she was, as you have said, very much a fool. Not quite a week ago she came here, with a bunch of storm troopers almost right behind her. The house was very active—Elsa has not been well since little Adolf was born last month—the doctor was here, and two nurses, with all the servants and children scurrying around.

By luck I answer the door. At first I think it is an old woman and then I see the face, and then I see the storm troopers have turned in the park gates. Can I hide her? It is one chance in thousands. A servant will be on us at any minute. Can I endure to have my house ransacked with Elsa ill in bed and to risk being arrested for harboring a Jew and to lose all I have built up here? Of course as a German I have one plain duty. She has displayed her Jewish body on the stage before pure young German men. I should hold her and turn her over to the storm troopers. But this I cannot do.

"You will destroy us all, Griselle," I tell her. "You must run back further in the park." She looks at me and smiles (she was always a brave girl) and makes her own choice.

"I would not bring you harm, Martin," she says, and she runs down the steps and out toward the trees. But she must be tired. She does not run very fast and the storm troopers have caught sight of her. I am helpless. I go in the house and in a few minutes she stops screaming, and in the morning I have the body sent down to the

100

village for burial. She was a fool to come to Germany. Poor little Griselle. I grieve with you, but as you see, I was helpless to aid her.

I must now demand you do not write again. Every word that comes to the house is now censored, and I cannot tell how soon they may start to open the mail to the bank. And I will no longer have any dealings with Jews, except for the receipt of money. It is not so good for me that a Jewess came here for refuge, and no further association can be tolerated.

A new Germany is being shaped here. We will soon show the world great things under our Glorious Leader.

Martin

Cablegram

MARTIN SCHULSE MUNICH JANUARY 2, 1934. YOUR TERMS ACCEPTED NOVEMBER TWELVE. AUDIT SHOWS THIRTEEN PERCENT INCREASE FEBRUARY SECOND FOURFOLD ASSURED PAN EXHIBITION MAY FIRST PREPARE LEAVE FOR MOSCOW IF MARKET OPENS UNEXPECTEDLY FINANCIAL INSTRUCTIONS MAILED NEW ADDRESS.   EISENSTEIN

Eisenstein Galleries
San Francisco, California
January 3, 1934.

Herrn Martin Schulse
Schloss Rantzenburg
Munich, Germany
Our dear Martin:

Don't forget grandma's birthday. She will be 64 on the 8th. American contributors will furnish 1000 brushes for your German Young Painters' League. Mandelberg has joined in supporting the league. You must send 11 Picasso reproductions, 20 by 90 to branch galleries on the 25th, no sooner. Reds and blues must predominate. We can allow

101

you $8000 on this transaction at present. Start new accounts book 2.
Our prayers follow you daily, dear brother,

Eisenstein

. Eisenstein Galleries
San Francisco, California
January 17, 1934.

Herrn Martin Schulse
Schloss Rantzenburg
Munich, Germany
Martin, dear brother:

Good news! Our stock reached 116 five days ago. The Fleishmans
have advanced another $10,000. This will fill your Young Painters'
League quota for a month but let us know if opportunities increase.
Swiss miniatures are having a vogue. You must watch the market and
plan to be in Zurich after May first if any unexpected opportunities
develop. Uncle Solomon will be glad to see you and I know you will
rely heavily on his judgment.

The weather is clear and there is little danger of storms during the
next two months. You will prepare for your students the following
reproductions: Van Gogh 15 by 103, red; Poussin 20 by 90, blue and
yellow; Vermeer 11 by 33, red and blue.

Our hopes will follow your new efforts.

Eisenstein

Eisenstein Galleries
San Francisco, California
January 29, 1934.

Dear Martin:

Your last letter was delivered by mistake at 457 Geary St., Room
4. Aunt Rheba says tell Martin he must write more briefly and clearly

so his friends can understand all that he says. I am sure everyone will be in readiness for your family reunion on the 15th. You will be tired after these festivities and may want to take your family with you on your trip to Zurich.

Before leaving, however, procure the following reproductions for branches of German Young Painters' League, looking forward to the joint exhibit in May or earlier: Picasso 17 by 81, red; Van Gogh 5 by 42, white; Rubens 15 by 204, blue and yellow.

Our prayers are with you
Eisenstein

Schloss Rantzenburg
Munich, Germany
February 12, 1934.

Mr. Max Eisenstein
Eisenstein Galleries
San Francisco, California, U.S.A.
Max, my old friend:

My God, Max, do you know what you do? I shall have to try to smuggle this letter out with an American I have met here. I write in appeal from a despair you cannot imagine. This crazy cable! These letters you have sent. I am called in to account for them. The letters are not delivered, but they bring me in and show me letters from you and demand I give them the code. A code? And how can you, a friend of long years, do this to me?

Do you realize, have you any idea that you destroy me? Already the results of your madness are terrible. I am bluntly told I must resign my office. Heinrich is no longer in the boys' corps. They tell him it will not be good for his health. God in heaven, Max, do you see what that means? And Elsa, to whom I dare not tell anything, comes in bewildered that the officials refuse her invitations and Baron Von Freische does not speak to her upon the street.

Yes, yes, I know why you do it—but do you not understand I could do nothing? What could I have done? I did not dare to try. I beg of you, not for myself, but for Elsa and the boys—think what it means to them if I am taken away and they do not know if I live or die. Do you know what it is to be taken to a concentration camp? Would you stand me against a wall and level the gun? I beg of you, stop. Stop now, while everything is not yet destroyed. I am in fear for my life, for my life, Max.

Is it you who does this? It cannot be you. I have loved you like a brother, my old Maxel. My God, have you no mercy? I beg you, Max, no more, no more! Stop while I can be saved. From a heart filled with old affection I ask it.

Martin

Eisenstein Galleries
San Francisco, California
February 15, 1934.

Herrn Martin Schulse
Schloss Rantzenburg
Munich, Germany
Our dear Martin:

Seven inches of rainfall here in 18 days. What a season! A shipment of 1500 brushes should reach the Berlin branch for your painters by this week end. This will allow time for practice before the big exhibition. American patrons will help with all the artists' supplies that can be provided, but you must make the final arrangements. We are too far out of touch with the European market and you are in a position to gauge the extent of support such a showing would arouse in

Germany. Prepare these for distribution by March 24th: Rubens 12 by 77, blue; Giotto 1 by 317, green and white; Poussin 20 by 90, red and white.

Young Blum left last Friday with the Picasso specifications. He will leave oils in Hamburg and Leipzig and will then place himself at your disposal.

Success to you!

Eisenstein

Eisenstein Galleries
San Francisco, California, U.S.A.
March 3, 1934.

Martin our brother:

Cousin Julius has two nine-pound boys. The family is happy. We regard the success of your coming artists' exhibition as assured. The last shipment of canvases was delayed due to difficulties of international exchange but will reach your Berlin associates in plenty of time. Consider reproduction collection complete. Your best support should come from Picasso enthusiasts but neglect no other lines.

We leave all final plans to your discretion but urge an early date for wholly successful exhibit.

The God of Moses be at your right hand.

Eisenstein

Kressmann Taylor

MY SIDE OF THE MATTER

Truman Capote

IT WAS IN THE MID-1940s when stories began coming to STORY *with some regularity from a young Southern writer, Truman Capote. These were increasingly interesting, so I began to write personal notes on our rejection slips, such banalities as, "This is interesting. Try us again," or "This came close. Keep trying," words an editor will use to encourage promising, but not yet publishable or professional writers. (I would add here, these few words do represent sincere interest on the part of a busy editor and should be taken with some seriousness.)*

"My Side of the Matter" came in on a day in which there had been little else of interest. After reading it twice I was so pleased I carried it from my office to those of the other editors, Whit, and Eleanor Gilchrist, our associate, announcing, "I think my boy has made it! Read this!"

They were charmed as I was, and we bought the story which, according to the author's statement at a cocktail party a year or so later, was the first story he sold professionally. Mademoiselle *magazine bought his second, but published theirs first, which gave rise to a silly situation about who "discovered" Capote. David Dempsey, a book columnist for the* New York Times, *got caught in the middle by publishing Capote's statement, and was scolded by the editors of* Mademoiselle. *The important fact is that here was a story teller, whose first stories still remain fresh and original. "My Side of the Matter," with its instinctive humor, tongue-in-cheek style, use of dialogue and soliloquy as a means of advancing the story, and the wicked simplicity of its ending, is still a favorite of mine.*

I know what is being said about me and you can take my side or theirs, that's your own business. It's my word against Eunice's and Olivia-Ann's and it should be plain enough to anyone with two good eyes which one of us has their wits about them. I just want the citizens of the U.S.A. to know the facts, that's all.

The facts: On Sunday, August 12, this year of our Lord, Eunice tried to kill me with her papa's Civil-War sword and Olivia-Ann cut up all over the place with a fourteen-inch hog knife. This is not even to mention lots of other things.

It began six months ago when I married Marge. That was the first thing I did wrong. We were married in Mobile after an acquaintance of only four days. We were both sixteen and she was visiting my cousin Georgia. Now that I've had plenty of time to think it over I can't for the life of me figure how I fell for the likes of her. She has no looks, no body, and no brains whatsoever. But Marge is a natural blonde and maybe that's the answer. Well, we were married going on three months when Marge ups and gets pregnant; the second thing I did wrong. Then she starts hollering that she's got to go home to Mama—only she hasn't got no mama, just these two aunts, Eunice and Olivia-Ann. So she makes me quit my perfectly swell position clerking at the Cash'n'Carry and move here to Admiral's Mill which is nothing but a damn gap in the road any way you care to consider it.

The day Marge and I got off the train at the L&N depot it was raining cats and dogs and do you think anyone came to meet us? I'd shelled out forty-one cents for a telegram too! Here my wife's pregnant and we have to tramp seven miles in a downpour. It was bad on Marge as I couldn't carry hardly any of our stuff on account of

I have terrible trouble with my back. When I first caught sight of this house I must say I was impressed. It's big and yellow and has real columns out in front and japonica trees, both red and white, lining the yard.

Eunice and Olivia-Ann had seen us coming and were waiting in the hall. I swear I wish you could get a look at these two. Honest, you'd die! Eunice is this big old fat thing with a behind that must weigh a tenth of a ton. She troops around the house, rain or shine, in this real old-fashioned nighty, calls it a kimono, but it isn't anything in this world but a dirty flannel nighty. Furthermore she chews tobacco and tries to pretend so lady-like, spitting on the sly. She keeps gabbing about what a fine education she had, which is her way of attempting to make me feel bad although, personally, it never bothers me so much as one whit as I know for a fact she can't even read the funnies without she spells out every single, solitary word. You've got to hand her one thing, though—she can add and subtract money so fast that there's no doubt but what she could be up in Washington, D.C., working where they make the stuff. Not that she hasn't got plenty of money! Naturally she says she hasn't but I know she has because one day, accidentally, I happened to find close to a thousand dollars hidden in a flower pot on the side porch. I didn't touch one cent only Eunice says I stole a hundred-dollar bill which is a venomous lie from start to finish. Of course anything Eunice says is an order from headquarters as not a breathing soul in Admiral's Mill can stand up and say he doesn't owe her money and if she said Charlie Carson (a blind, ninety-year-old invalid, who hasn't taken a step since 1896) threw her on her back and raped her everybody in this county would swear the same on a stack of Bibles.

Now Olivia-Ann is worse, and that's the truth! Only she's not so bad on the nerves as Eunice for she is a natural-born half-wit and ought really to be kept in somebody's attic. She's real pale and skinny and has a mustache. She squats around most the time whittling on a stick with her fourteen-inch hog knife, otherwise she's up to some devilment, like what she did to Mrs. Harry Steller Smith. I swore not ever to tell anyone that, but when a vicious attempt has been made on a person's life, I say the hell with promises.

Mrs. Harry Steller Smith was Eunice's canary named after a woman from Pensacola who makes homemade cure-all that Eunice takes for the gout. One day I heard this terrible racket in the parlor and upon investigating, what did I find but Olivia-Ann shooing Mrs. Harry Steller Smith out an open window with a broom and the door to the bird cage wide. If I hadn't walked in at exactly that moment she might never have been caught. She got scared that I would tell Eunice and blurted out the whole thing, said it wasn't fair to keep one of God's creatures locked up that way, besides which she couldn't stand Mrs. Harry Steller Smith's singing. Well, I felt kind of sorry for her and she gave me two dollars, so I helped her cook up a story for Eunice. Of course I wouldn't have taken the money except I thought it would ease her conscience.

The very *first* words Eunice said when I stepped inside this house were, "So this is what you ran off behind our backs and married, Marge?"

Marge says, "Isn't he the best-looking thing, Aunt Eunice?"

Eunice eyes me u-p and d-o-w-n and says, "Tell him to turn around."

While my back is turned, Eunice says, "You sure must've picked the runt of the litter. Why, this isn't any sort of man at all."

I've never been so taken back in my life! True, I'm slightly stocky, but then I haven't got my full growth yet.

"He is too," says Marge.

Olivia-Ann, who's been standing there with her mouth so wide the flies could buzz in and out, says, "You heard what Sister said. He's not any sort of a man whatsoever. The very idea of this little runt running around claiming to be a man! Why, he isn't even of the male sex!"

Marge says, "You seem to forget, Aunt Olivia-Ann, that this is my husband, the father of my unborn child."

Eunice made a nasty sound like only she can and said, "Well, all I can say is I most certainly wouldn't be bragging about it."

Isn't that a nice welcome? And after I gave up my perfectly swell position clerking at the Cash'n'Carry.

But it's not a drop in the bucket to what came later that same evening. After Bluebell cleared away the supper dishes, Marge asked, just as nice as she could, if we could borrow the car and drive over to the picture show at Phoenix City.

"You must be clear out of your head," says Eunice and honest you'd think we'd asked for the kimono off her back.

"You must be clear out of your head," says Olivia-Ann.

"It's six o'clock," says Eunice, "and if you think I'd let that runt drive my just as good as brand-new 1934 Chevrolet as far as the privy and back you must've gone clear out of your head."

Naturally such language makes Marge cry.

"Never you mind, honey," I said, "I've driven pu-lenty of Cadillacs in my time."

"Humf," says Eunice. "Yeah," says I.

Eunice says, "If he's ever so much as driven a plow I'll eat a dozen gophers fried in turpentine."

"I won't have you refer to my husband in any such manner," says Marge. "You're acting simply outlandish! Why, you'd think I'd picked up some absolutely strange man in some absolutely strange place."

"If the shoe fits, wear it!" says Eunice.

"Don't think you can pull the sheep over our eyes," says Olivia-Ann in that braying voice of hers so much like the mating call of a jackass you can't rightly tell the difference.

"We weren't born just around the corner, you know," says Eunice.

Marge says, "I'll give you to understand that I'm legally wed till death do us part to this man by a certified justice of the peace as of three and one-half months ago. Ask anybody. Furthermore, Aunt

Eunice, he is free, white and sixteen. Furthermore, George Far Sylvester does not appreciate hearing his father referred to in any such manner."

George Far Sylvester is the name we've planned for the baby. Has a strong sound, don't you think? Only the way things stand I have positively no feelings in the matter now whatsoever.

"How can a girl have a baby with a girl?" says Olivia-Ann, which was a calculated attack on my manhood. "I do declare there's something new every day."

"Oh, shush up," says Eunice. "Let us hear no more about the picture show in Phoenix City."

Marge sobs, "Oh-h-h, but it's Judy Garland."

"Never mind, honey," I said, "I most likely saw the show in Mobile ten years ago."

"That's a deliberate falsehood," shouts Olivia-Ann. "Oh, you are a scoundrel, you are. Judy hasn't been in the pictures ten years." Olivia-Ann's never seen not even one picture show in her entire fifty-two years (she won't tell anybody how old she is but I dropped a card to the capitol in Montgomery and they were very nice about answering) but she subscribes to eight movie books. According to Postmistress Delancey it's the only mail she ever gets outside of the Sears & Roebuck. She has this positively morbid crush on Gary Cooper and has one trunk and two suitcases full of his photos.

So we got up from the table and Eunice lumbers over to the window and looks out to the chinaberry tree and says, "Birds settling in their roost—time we went to bed. You have your old room, Marge, and I've fixed a cot for this gentleman on the back porch."

It took a solid minute for that to sink in.

I said, "And what, if I'm not too bold to ask, is the objection to my sleeping with my lawful wife?"

Then they both started yelling at me.

So Marge threw a conniption fit right then and there, "Stop it, stop it, stop it! I can't stand anymore. Go on, baby-doll . . . go on and sleep wherever they say. Tomorrow we'll see. . . ."

Eunice says, "I swanee if the child hasn't got a grain of sense after all."

"Poor dear," says Olivia-Ann, wrapping her arm around Marge's waist and herding her off. "Poor dear, so young, so innocent. Let's us just go and have a good cry on Olivia-Ann's shoulder."

May, June, July and the best part of August I've squatted and sweltered on that damn back porch without an ounce of screening. And Marge—she hasn't opened her mouth in protest, not once! This part of Alabama is swampy, with mosquitoes that could murder a buffalo given half a chance, not to mention dangerous flying roaches and a posse of local rats big enough to haul a wagon train from here to Timbuctoo. Oh, if it wasn't for that little unborn George I would've been making dust tracks on the road, way before now. I mean to say I haven't had five seconds alone with Marge since that first night. One or the other is always chaperoning and last week they like to have blown their tops when Marge locked herself in her room and they couldn't find me nowhere. The truth is I'd been down watching the niggers bale cotton but just for spite I let on to Eunice like Marge and I'd been up to no good. After that they added Bluebell to the shift.

And all this time I haven't even had cigarette change.

Eunice has hounded me day in and day out about getting a job. "Why don't the little heathen go out and get some honest work?" says she. As you've probably noticed, she never speaks to me directly, though more often than not I am the only one in her royal presence. "If he was any sort of man you could call a man he'd be trying to put a crust of bread in that girl's mouth instead of stuffing his own off my vittles." I think you should know that I've been living almost exclusively on cold yams and leftover grits for three months and thirteen days and I've been down to consult Dr. A. N. Carter twice. He's not exactly sure whether I have the scurvy or not.

And as for my not working, I'd like to know what a man of my abilities, a man who held a perfectly swell position with the Cash'n'-

113

Carry, would find to do in a flea-bag like Admiral's Mill? There is all of one store here and Mr. Tubberville, the proprietor, is actually so lazy it's painful for him to have to sell anything. Then we have the Morning Star Baptist Church but they already have a preacher, an awful old character named Shell whom Eunice drug over one day to see about the salvation of my soul. I heard him with my own ears tell her I was too far gone.

But it's what Eunice has done to Marge that really takes the cake. She has turned that girl against me in the most villainous fashion that words could not describe. Why, she even reached the point where she was sassing me back, but I provided her with a couple of good slaps and put a stop to that. No wife of mine is ever going to be disrespectful to me, not on your life.

The enemy lines are stretched tight: Bluebell, Olivia-Ann, Eunice, Marge, and the whole rest of Admiral's Mill (pop. 342). Allies, none. Such was the situation as of Sunday, August 12, when the attempt was made upon my very life.

Yesterday was quiet and hot enough to melt rock. The trouble began at exactly two o'clock. I know because Eunice has one of those fool cuckoo contraptions and it scares the daylights out of me. I was minding my own personal business in the parlor composing a song on the upright piano which Eunice bought for Olivia-Ann and hired her a teacher to come all the way from Columbus, Georgia, once a week. Postmistress Delancey, who was my friend till she decided that it was maybe not so wise, says that the fancy teacher tore out of this house one afternoon like old Adolf Hitler was on his tail and leaped in his Ford coupé, never to be heard from again. Like I say, I'm trying to keep cool in the parlor not bothering a living soul when Olivia-Ann trots in with her hair all twisted up in curlers, and shrieks, "Cease that infernal racket this very instant! Can't you give a body a minute's rest? And get off my piano right smart. It's not your piano, it's my piano and if you don't get off it right smart I'll have you in court like a shot the first Monday in September."

She's not anything in this world but jealous on account of I'm a natural-born musician and the songs I make up out of my own head are absolutely marvelous.

"And just look what you've done to my genuine ivory keys, Mr. Sylvester," says she, trotting over to the piano. "Torn nearly every one of them off right at the roots for purentee meanness, that's what you've done."

She knows good and well that the piano was ready for the junk heap the moment I entered this house.

I said, "Seeing as you're such a know-it-all, Miss Olivia-Ann, maybe it would interest you to know that I'm in the possession of a few interesting tales myself. A few things that maybe other people would be very grateful to know. Like what happened to Mrs. Harry Steller Smith, as for instance."

Remember Mrs. Harry Steller Smith?

She paused and looked at the empty bird cage. "You gave me your oath," says she and turned the most terrifying shade of purple.

"Maybe I did and again maybe I didn't," says I. "You did an evil thing when you betrayed Eunice that way but if some people will leave other people alone then maybe I can overlook it."

Well sir, she walked out of there just as *nice* and *quiet* as you please. So I went and stretched out on the sofa which is the most horrible piece of furniture I've ever seen and is part of a matched set Eunice bought in Atlanta in 1912 and paid two thousand dollars for, cash— or so she claims. This set is black and olive plush and smells like wet chicken feathers on a damp day. There is a big table in one corner of the parlor which supports two pictures of Miss E and O-A's mama and papa. Papa is kind of handsome but just between you and me I'm convinced he has black blood in him somewhere. He was a captain in the Civil War and that is one thing I'll never forget on account of his sword which is displayed over the mantel and figures prominently in the action yet to come. Mama has that hangdog, half-wit look like Olivia-Ann though I must say Mama carries it better.

So I had just about dozed off when I heard Eunice bellowing, "Where is he? Where is he?" And the next thing I know she's framed

115

in the doorway with her hands planted plump on those hippo hips and the whole pack scrunched up behind her: Bluebell, Olivia-Ann and Marge.

Several seconds passed with Eunice tapping her big old bare foot just as fast and furious as she could and fanning her fat face with this cardboard picture of Niagara Falls.

"Where is it?" says she. "Where's my hundred dollars that he made away with while my trusting back was turned?"

"*This* is the straw that broke the camel's back," says I, but I was too hot and tired to get up.

"That's not the only back that's going to be broke," says she, her bug eyes about to pop clear out of their sockets. "That was my funeral money and I want it back. Wouldn't you know he'd steal from the dead?"

"Maybe he didn't take it," says Marge.

"You keep your mouth out of this, missy," says Olivia-Ann.

"He stole my money sure as shooting," says Eunice. "Why, look at his eyes . . . black with guilt!"

I yawned and said, "Like they say in the courts . . . if the party of the first part falsely accuses the party of the second part then the party of the first part can be locked away in jail even if the State Home is where they rightfully belong for the protection of all concerned."

"God will punish him," says Eunice.

"Oh, Sister," says Olivia-Ann, "let us not wait for God."

Whereupon Eunice advances on me with this most peculiar look, her dirty flannel nighty jerking along the floor. And Olivia-Ann leeches after her and Bluebell lets forth this moan that must have been heard clear to Eufala and back while Marge stands there wringing her hands and whimpering.

"Oh-h-h," sobs Marge, "please give her back the money, baby-doll."

I said, "*Et tu, Brute?*" which is from William Shakespeare.

"Look at the likes of him," says Eunice, "lying around all day not doing so much as licking a postage stamp."

"Pitiful," clucks Olivia-Ann.

"You'd think he was having a baby instead of that poor child." Eunice speaking.

Bluebell tosses in her two cents, "Ain't it the truth?"

"Well, if it isn't the old pots calling the kettle black," says I.

"After loafing here for three months, does this runt have the audacity to cast aspersions in my direction?" says Eunice.

I merely flicked a bit of ash from my sleeve and not the least bit fazed, said, "Dr. A. N. Carter has informed me that I am in a dangerous scurvy condition and can't stand the least excitement whatsoever —otherwise I'm liable to foam at the mouth and bite somebody."

Then Bluebell says, "Why don't he go back to that trash in Mobile, Miss Eunice? I'se sick an' tired of carryin' his ol' slop jar."

Naturally that coal-black character made me so mad I couldn't see straight.

So just as calm as a cucumber I arose and picked up this umbrella off the hat tree and rapped her across the head with it until it cracked smack in two.

"My real Japanese silk parasol!" shrieks Olivia-Ann.

Marge cries, "You've killed Bluebell, you've killed poor old Bluebell!"

Eunice shoves Olivia-Ann and says, "He's gone clear out of his head, Sister! Run! Run and get Mr. Tubberville!"

"I don't like Mr. Tubberville," says Olivia-Ann staunchly. "I'll go get my hog knife." And she makes a dash for the door but seeing as I care nothing for death I brought her down with a sort of tackle. It wrenched my back something terrible.

"He's going to kill her!" hollers Eunice loud enough to bring the goose down. "He's going to murder us all! I warned you, Marge. Quick, child, get Papa's sword!"

So Marge gets Papa's sword and hands it to Eunice. Talk about wifely devotion! And if that's not bad enough, Olivia-Ann gives me this terrific knee punch and I had to let go. The next thing you know we hear her out in the yard bellowing hymns.

"Mine eyes have seen the glory of the coming of the Lord.
He is tramping out the vintage where the grapes of
wrath are stored . . ."

Meanwhile Eunice is sashaying all over the place wildly thrashing Papa's sword and somehow I've managed to clamber atop the piano. Then Eunice climbs up on the piano stool and how that rickety contraption survived a monster like her I'll never be the one to tell.

"Come down from there, you yellow coward, before I run you through," says she and takes a whack and I've got a half-inch cut to prove it.

By this time Bluebell has recovered and skittered away to join Olivia-Ann holding services in the front yard. I guess they were expecting my body and God knows it would've been theirs if Marge hadn't passed out cold.

That's the only good thing I've got to say for Marge.

What happened after that I can't rightly remember except for Olivia-Ann reappearing with her fourteen-inch hog knife and a bunch of the neighbors. But suddenly Marge was the star attraction and I suppose they carried her to her room. Anyway, as soon as they left I barricaded the parlor door.

I've got all those black and olive plush chairs pushed against it and that big mahogany table that must weigh a couple of tons and the hat tree and lots of other stuff. I've locked the windows and pulled down the shades. Also I've found a five-pound box of Sweet Love candy and this very minute I'm munching a juicy, creamy, chocolate cherry. Oh yes, they've started singing a song of a very different color. But as for me—I give them a tune on the piano every now and then just to let them know I'm cheerful.

THE IMPORTANT THING

Tennessee Williams

THE SHORT STORY has always been close to the theater, to drama. In a volume Whit and I edited in the early 1950s, STORY: The Fiction of the Forties, *we discovered a curious thing: more than a third of the authors in the book were also writing plays, and in two cases plays developed from the short stories we had published. And TV came later.*

When Tennessee Williams's story "The Important Thing" came in to STORY *in the 1940s, he was already one of our most distinguished and exciting living American dramatists. This was not his first story in our magazine; but when an earlier one had been submitted some years before, he was, according to Whit, "a young man who had just completed a bicycle trip through Mexico. Like all writers then he was broke, but already he'd had a couple of one-act plays produced, and was working on his first full-length. At the moment, however, he was washing dishes in a restaurant for his board."*

Ten or fifteen years later Whit and I and our two children, John and Whitney, went over to Paris on the S.S. United States, *and Tennessee was also on board ship on his way to Italy. Lionized—and dancing with Joan Crawford (on her honeymoon) the first night we saw him—he was glad to see Whit, and after this, we spent evenings with him and two of his good friends, a brother and sister on their way to St. Malo, France.*

Good talk; and yet I remember Tennessee was above all concerned about the success or failure of his new play Cat on a Hot Tin Roof. *"A born writer," wrote Whit, "is almost always a born worrier!"*

This story, "The Important Thing," is one that probably could not have been done so well by any other writer. Here is the author's principal theme, apparent in all his works—the sadness of defeated relationships and the poetry there is in dreams. It also shows the author's knowledge of what a story is all about.

They met at the spring dance by the Baptist Female College which Laura was attending that year. The college was in the same town as the state university at which John was completing his sophomore year. He knew only one girl at the college and wasn't able to find her in the ballroom. It was hot and crowded and had that feverish, glaring effect which usually prevails at a spring dance given by a sectarian girls' school. The room was lighted by four or five blazing chandeliers and the walls were covered with long mirrors. Between dances the couples stood about stiffly in their unaccustomed formal dress and glanced uneasily at the reflection in the highly polished glass, shifted their weight from foot to foot, nervously twisted or flipped their program cards. None of them seemed to know each other very well. They talked in loud, unnatural voices, shrieked with laughter or stood sullenly quiet. The teachers flitted among them with birdlike alacrity, intently frowning or beaming, introducing, prompting, encouraging. It was not like a social affair. It was more like an important military maneuver.

John walked around the edge of the floor several times and was rather relieved at not finding the one girl he knew. When he arrived at the palm-flanked entrance he turned to go out, but just then his arm was violently plucked by one of the teachers, a middle-aged woman with frowzy gray hair, sharp nose, and large yellow teeth.

She looked so wild and Harpy-like that John involuntarily squirmed aside from her grasp.

"Are you alone?" she shrieked in his ear.

The band was thumping out a terrifically loud foxtrot. John rubbed his ear and pointed vaguely toward the door. But she tightened her grasp on his arm and propelled him across the floor by a series of jerks that careened him from one dancing couple to another till they reached a corner where stood an apparently stranded group of young Baptist females beneath the protective fronds of an enormous boxed palm.

The Harpy gave his arm a final twist and John found himself facing a tall, thin girl in a pink taffeta dress who stood slightly apart from her fellow refugees. He caught the name Laura shrieked through the increasing din. He didn't notice the girl's face. He was too furious at being roped in like this even to look at her. They advanced awkwardly toward each other. John slid his arm around her unbelievably slender waist. Through the silk he could feel the hard ridge of her spine. There was no weight to her body. She floated before him so lightly that it was almost like dancing by himself, except that the cord of bone kept moving beneath his warm, sweating fingers and her fine, loose hair plastered itself against his damp cheek.

The foxtrot had reached a crescendo. Cymbals were clashing and drums beating out double time. The girl's lips moved against his throat. Her breath tickled his skin but he couldn't hear a word she was saying. He looked helplessly down at her. Suddenly she broke away from him. She stood slightly off from him, her eyes crinkling with laughter and one hand clutched to her mouth. The music stopped.

"What're you laughing at?" John asked.

"The whole situation," said Laura. "You no more wanted to dance than I did!"

"Didn't you want to?"

"Of course not. When I think of dancing I think of Isadora Dun-

121

can who said she wanted to teach the whole world how to dance, but this wasn't what she meant—do you think it was?"

She had a way of looking up that made her face very brilliant and for a few moments obscured the fact that she was by no means pretty. But there was something about her, something which already excited him a little, and so he said, "Let's go outside."

They spent practically all the rest of the evening in the oak grove between the gymnasium and the chapel, strolling around and smoking his cigarettes. While smoking the girl would flatten herself against a tree trunk, for smoking was forbidden on the campus.

"This is the advantage of being a fence pole," she told him. "You can hide behind anything with the slightest diameter."

Everything that she said had a wry, humorous twist, and even when it wasn't humorous she would laugh slightly and John had the impression that she was unusually clever. They went into the empty chapel for a while and sat in a back pew and talked about religion.

"It's all so archaic," Laura said. "It's all a museum piece!"

John had recently become an agnostic himself. They agreed that the Christian religion and the Hebrew, in fact, nearly all religions, were based on a concept of guilt.

"*Mea culpa!*" said John, thinking that she would say, "What's that?" But she didn't. She nodded her head. And he was excited to discover that she, too, was interested in writing. She had won a literary prize in high school and she was now editor of the college literary magazine. The teacher who had brought them together was Laura's English instructor.

"She thinks I'm very talented," said Laura. "She wants me to send one of my stories to *Harper's.*"

"Why don't you?" asked John.

"Oh, I don't know," said Laura. "I think the main thing is just expressing yourself as honestly as you can. I am not interested in style," she went on, "it's such a waste of time to do things over and get the right cadence and always just the right word. I'd rather just scramble through one thing and then rush into another, until I have said everything that I have to say!"

How extraordinary it was that she and John should feel exactly the same way about this! He confessed that he was himself a writer and that two or three of his stories were coming out in the university's literary magazine—and when Laura heard this she was almost absurdly moved.

"I'd love to see them, I've got to see them!" she cried.

"I'll bring them over," he promised.

"When?"

"As soon as they come out!"

"I don't care how the style is as long as they're honest. They've got to be honest!" she pleaded. "Are they?"

"I hope so," he answered uneasily.

She had taken his arm and was squeezing it in a grip that was almost as tight as a wrestler's, and with every excited inflection in her speech she squeezed it tighter. There was no relaxation in Laura, none of the softness and languor which he found physically interesting in girls. He could not imagine her lying passively still and quietly submitting the way he thought a girl should to a man's embraces.

"What do you think about human relations?" she asked him just at the moment when this disturbing image was in his mind.

"That's a large subject," said John.

"Oh, what a large, large subject! And it is the one I will never be able to cope with!"

"Why?" asked John.

"I'm equal to anything else, but not human relations! I'll always be moving when other people are still, and still when they're moving," said Laura, "and it will be a terrible mess and a mix-up from start to finish!"

"You shouldn't feel that way about it," he told her lamely, astonished at the way her words fitted exactly what he had been thinking.

She looked up at John. "You'll have the same trouble!" she told him. "We'll never be happy but we'll have lots of excitement, and if we hold on to our personal integrity everything won't be lost!"

He wasn't quite sure what Laura was talking about, and personal integrity seemed the vaguest of terms. Was it something like what she meant by "honest" writing?

"Yes, something," said Laura, "but ever so much more difficult, because writing is ideal reality and living is not ideal. . . ."

At the window of the gymnasium they stood for a while and watched the dancers who had reached what appeared to be nearly the point of exhaustion. Faces that had been flushed and perspiring when they had left the room were now quite desperate-looking and the men in the jazz band seemed to be playing now out of sheer inability to break an old habit. Some of the paper streamers had come unfastened and fallen upon the floor, others hung limply from the ceiling, and in one corner a small crowd, mostly teachers, were clustered about a girl who had fainted.

"Don't they look silly!" said Laura.

"Who?"

"Dancers—everybody!"

"What isn't silly, in your opinion?" asked John.

"Give me a little while to answer that question!"

"How long shall I give you?"

"I'll tell you right now—The Important Thing isn't silly!"

"What Important Thing?" John asked.

"I don't know yet," said Laura. "Why do you think I'm living, except to discover what The Important Thing is?"

John didn't see her again that spring. Final examinations came soon after the dance, and besides he was not altogether sure that she was the sort of girl he would get along with. She was not good-looking and her intensity which was so charming while he was with her seemed afterward a little fantastic.

Very soon after he returned to school that fall he ran into her on the campus. She was now enrolled as a sophomore in the state university. He barely recognized her. It had been so dark in the oak grove, where they spent most of their time at the spring dance, that he hadn't gotten a very clear impression of her face. She was at once homelier and more attractive than he remembered. Her face was very wide at the top and narrow at the bottom: almost an inverted pyramid. Her eyes were large and rather oblique, hazel brown with startling flecks of blue or green in them. Her nose was long and pointed and the tip covered with freckles. She had a way of smiling and blinking her eyes very rapidly as she talked. She talked so fast and shrilly that he felt a little embarrassed. He noticed a group of girls staring at her and giggling. Fools, he thought, and was angry at himself for having felt embarrassed.

It was noon when they met and she was on her way to the boardinghouse where she was staying. She hadn't pledged a sorority. She announced the fact with an air of proud defiance that John liked.

"I could see that I wouldn't fit into any of them," she said. "I'd rather be independent, wouldn't you? The trouble with this world is that everybody has to compromise and conform. Oh, I'm sick of it! I won't do it! I shall live my own life just the way that I please!"

John had felt the same way about joining a fraternity and he told her so.

"Ah, we're a couple of barbs!" she shrieked. "Isn't that marvelous? The other girls at the boardinghouse simply detest being called barbs —but I adore it! I think it's really thrilling to be called a barbarian! It makes you feel like you could strip off your clothes and dance naked in the streets if you felt like doing it!"

John felt a warm glow as though he'd been drinking. It was the way he'd felt in the oak grove, talking to her last spring. It seemed suddenly that he had a great deal to say. He became excited and started talking rapidly about a one-act play that he was writing. It was full of involved symbolism and hard to explain. But Laura nodded her head with quick, eager jerks and supplied words wherever he stumbled. She seemed to know intuitively what he was trying to say.

"Oh, I think that's marvelous, marvelous!" she kept repeating.

He was thinking of submitting it to the one-act play contest. His roommate had urged him to do so.

"My goodness, why don't you!" exclaimed Laura.

"Oh, I don't know," John said. "I think the main thing is just expressing oneself, don't you?"

Immediately afterward they both laughed, remembering that Laura had said the same thing about the story her English teacher had wanted her to send to *Harper's*.

"Was it accepted?" John asked.

"No, it came back with a printed card," she admitted ruefully. "But I don't care. I'm writing poetry now. They say that you should write poetry while you're young and feel things keenly."

She laughed and caught John's arm. "I feel things very keenly, don't you?"

They sat down on the front steps of the boardinghouse and talked until the bell tolled for one-o'clock classes. Both of them had missed their lunch.

They saw a great deal of each other after that. They had many interests in common. They were both on the staff of the university's literary magazine and belonged to the Poetry and French clubs. It was the year of the national election and John became twenty-one just in time to vote. Laura spent hours arguing with him about politics and finally convinced him that he must vote for Norman Thomas. Later they both joined the Young Communists' League. John became a very enthusiastic radical. He helped operate a secret printing press and distribute pamphlets about the campus attacking fraternities, political control of the university, academic conservatism, and so forth. He was once called before the dean of men and threatened with expulsion. Laura thought this was terribly thrilling.

"If you get expelled," she promised, "I'll quit school too!"

But it all blew over and they both remained in the university.

All of these things served to draw them closer together. But for some reason they were not altogether at ease with each other. John always had the feeling that something very important was going to happen between them. He could not have explained why he felt that way. Perhaps it was the contagion of Laura's intensity. When he was with her he felt the kind of suppressed excitement a scientist might feel upon the verge of an important discovery. A constant expectation or suspense. Was Laura conscious of the same thing? Sometimes he felt sure that she was. But her enthusiasm was so diffuse that he could never be sure. One thing after another caught her interest. She was like a precocious child just discovering the world, taking nothing in it for granted, receiving each impression with the fresh wonder of a child but an adult's mature understanding. About most things she talked very frankly. But once in a while she would become oddly reticent.

Once he asked her where she came from.

"Kansas," she told him.

"I know, but what place in Kansas?"

He was surprised to see her face coloring. They were in the reference room of the library that evening, studying together at one of the yellow oak tables. She opened her notebook and ignored his question.

"What place?" he insisted, wondering why she flushed.

Abruptly she slammed the notebook shut and faced him with a laugh. "What does it matter what place?"

"I just wanted to know."

"Well, I won't tell you!"

"Why not?"

"Because it doesn't matter where you come from. It only matters where you're going!"

"Where are you going, then?"

"I don't know!"

She leaned back in the straight yellow oak chair and shook with laughter. "How on earth should I know where I'm going?"

The librarian approached them with a warning frown. "Please, not so loud. This room's for study."

"Where are you going?" John repeated under his breath.

127

Laura hid her face in the notebook and continued laughing.

"Where are you going, where are you going, where are you going!" John whispered. He did it to tease her. She looked so funny with the black leather notebook covering her face, only her braided hair showing and her throat flushed turkey red.

All at once she jumped up from the table and he saw that her face was contorted with crying. She rushed out of the room and he couldn't get her to speak a word to him all the way back to her boardinghouse.

Some time later he found the name of her home town on the envelope of a letter which she'd forgotten to remove from a book of poems she'd loaned him. The envelope was postmarked from Hardwood, Kansas. John grinned. It was a hick town in the northwestern part of the state and probably the deadest spot on earth. . . .

Despising himself for doing so, he opened the letter and read it. It was from Laura's mother and was a classic of its kind. It complained of the money Laura was having to spend on board and books, urged her to spend less time writing nonsense and buckle down to hard work so that she could get a teaching job when she got through with her schooling because times were getting to be very bad. . . . "The ground and the people and the business and everything else is dried up around here," wrote the mother. "I don't know what things are coming to. It must be God's judgment, I guess. Three solid years of drought. Looks like this time God is planning to dry the wickedness out of the world instead of drowning it out!"

That spring John bought a used car for thirty-five dollars and every free afternoon he and Laura drove around the lovely country roads and had picnic lunches which Laura prepared. He was getting used to Laura's odd appearance and her absurd animation, but other people weren't. She had become something of a character on the campus. John was at this time being rushed by a professional fraternity and he was told that some of the fellows thought that Laura was a very queer person for him to be seen around with. Now and again his mind would go back to their first conversation in the oak grove of the Baptist Female College, the talk about human relations and her inability to cope with them, and it appeared to him that she was not even going halfway in attempting to. There was no reason for her to talk so loudly on such eclectic subjects whenever they passed along a crowded corridor of a university building, there was surely no reason for her to be so rude to people she wasn't interested in, walking abruptly away without an excuse when talk turned to things she classified as inane—which was almost everything John's other friends talked about.

Other girls on the campus he could look at and imagine in the future, settled down into average middle-class life, becoming teachers or entering other professions. But when he looked at Laura he could not see her future, he could not imagine her becoming or doing any known thing, or going back to Hardwood, Kansas, or going anywhere else. She did not fit happily or comfortably into the university cosmos, but in what other place or circumstances—he asked himself —could she have found any refuge whatsoever? Perhaps he was no more like other people than she was, but his case was different. He was more adaptable, he demanded a good deal less of people and things. Come up against a barrier, he was of a nature to look for a way around it. But Laura—

Laura had decided that the English department of the university was hopelessly reactionary and the only course she took an interest in, now, was geology. Their favorite spot, that spring, was an abandoned rock quarry where Laura searched for fossils. She danced around the quarry like a bright, attractive little monkey on a wire, her green smock fluttering in the wind and her voice constantly flowing up to him, sometimes shrill with excitement and sometimes muted with intense absorption.

"Don't you ever want to be still?" John asked her.

"Never till I have to!"

John would get tired of waiting and would open the lunch box. She would finally join him on the hilltop, too tired to eat, and would spread her fossils around her and pore delightedly over them while John munched sandwiches of peanut butter and jelly or Swiss cheese on rye. The rest of the afternoon they would spend talking about literature and life, art and civilization. They both had tremendous admiration for the ancient Greeks and the modern Russians. Greece is the world's past, said Laura, and Russia is the future—which John thought a brilliant statement, though it sounded a little familiar as if he had come across it somewhere before in a book.

Their discussions would continue unflaggingly till sundown, but as dusk began to settle they would become a little nervous and constrained, for some reason, and there would be long pauses in their talk, during which it was curiously difficult for them to look at each other. After a while, when it was getting really dark, Laura would abruptly jump up from the grass and brush off her smock. "I guess we'd better be going," she would say. Her voice would sound with the dull, defeated tone of someone who has argued a long time about something very important without making any impression upon the other's mind. John would feel strangely miserable as he followed her down the hill to where they had parked the old roadster. He would also feel that something had been left unsaid or undone, a feeling of incompletion. . . .

It was the last Saturday before the end of the spring term. They were going to spend the whole day out in the country, studying for a final examination in a French course which they were taking together. Laura had prepared sandwiches and deviled eggs. And John, with some trepidation, had purchased a quart of red wine. He put the bottle in the side pocket of the roadster and didn't mention it until after they'd finished eating because he knew Laura didn't like drinking. She had no moral objections, she said, but thought it was a senseless, wasteful practice. She refused to drink any of the wine. "But you may, if you wish," she added with a primness that made John laugh.

They were seated, as usual, on the grassy hill above the rock quarry. It was called Lover's Leap. Laura held the notebook which they had prepared together and was quizzing John. She was leaning against one of the large white boulders scattered about the hilltop and John was stretched at her feet. He held the wine bottle between his knees and drank out of the thermos cup. Laura's constraint at first sight of the bottle wore off. She called him Bacchus.

"I wish I had time to make you a wreath," she said. "You'd look too adorable with a wreath of green leaves!"

"Why don't you be a nymph?" John asked. "Take off your clothes and be a wood nymph! I'll chase you through the birch trees!"

The idea pleased John very much. He laughed loudly. But Laura was embarrassed. She cleared her throat and held the notebook in front of her face, but he could see by the base of her throat that she was blushing. He stopped laughing, feeling somewhat embarrassed himself. He knew what she was thinking. She was thinking what might happen if he should catch her among the birch trees with all her clothes off. . . .

John drank another cupful of wine. He felt very good. He had removed his jacket and unbuttoned the collar of his shirt and rolled up the sleeves. The sun shone dazzlingly in his eyes, made rainbows in his eyelashes, warmed the bare flesh of his throat and arms. A comfortable glow passed through him. He was newly conscious of the life in his body; flexed his legs, rubbed his stomach, and arched his thighs. He no longer listened to the questions that Laura was asking him out of the notebook. She had to repeat them two or three times before they were clear.

At last she became disgusted and tossed the notebook aside. "I believe you're getting intoxicated!" she told him sharply.

He looked indolently up at her. "Maybe I am! What of it?"

He noticed that she was not very pretty. Especially not when she drew her brows together and squinted her eyes like that. Her face was irregular and bony-looking. Rather outlandish, so broad at the top and narrow at the bottom. Long pointed nose and eyes flecked with different colors which were too large for the rest of her and always filled with superfluous brightness. Reminded him of an undersized child he once knew in grammar school. For some reason they called him Peekie and threw rocks at him after school. A timid, ridiculous creature with a high, squeaky voice that everyone mocked. The larger boys caught him after school and asked him the meaning of obscene words or pulled the buttons off his knickers. She was like that. A queer person. But there was something exciting about her just as there'd been something exciting about Peekie that made the larger boys want to amuse themselves with him. There was something about her that he wanted to set his hands on in a rough way—twist and pull and tease! Her skin was the most attractive thing about her. It was very fine and smooth and white. . . .

John's eyes traveled down her body. She wore a black sweater and a black-and-white checked skirt. As he looked at her legs a brisk wind tossed her skirt up and he could see the bare flesh above where the stockings ended. He rolled over on his stomach and placed both hands on her thighs. He'd never touched her so intimately before but somehow it seemed a perfectly natural thing to do. She made a startled movement away from him. Suddenly he thought he knew what the important thing was that was going to happen between them. He caught her by the shoulders and tried to pull her down in the grass, but she fought against him wildly. Neither of them said anything. They just fought together like two wild animals, rolling in the grass and clawing at each other. Laura clawed at John's face and John clawed at Laura's body. They accepted this thing, this desperate battle between them, as though they'd known all along it was coming, as though it had been inevitable from the start. Neither of them spoke a word until they were at last exhausted and lay still on the grass, breathing heavily and looking up at the slowly darkening sky.

John's face was scratched and bleeding in several places. Laura pressed her hands against her stomach and groaned. He had kicked her with his knee trying to make her lie still.

"It's all over now," he said. "I'm not going to hurt you."

But she continued moaning.

The sun had gone down and dusk gathered. There was a big, purplish-red blotch in the western sky that looked like a bruised place.

John got up to his feet and stood silently staring at the angry afterglow. Away off to the left was the university town, beginning to emerge through its leafy clouds with the sparkling animation of a Saturday night in late spring. There would be many gay parties and dances that night. Girls in dresses that seemed to be woven of flowers would whirl about polished dance floors and couples would whisper and laugh behind clumps of ghostly spirea. These were the natural celebrations of youth. He and this girl had been searching for something else. What was it? Again and again later on the search would be made, the effort to find something outside of common experience, digging and rooting among the formless rubble of things for the one lost thing that was altogether lovely—and perhaps every time a repetition of this, violence and ugliness of desire turned to rage. . . .

He spoke aloud to himself. "We didn't have anything—we were fooling ourselves."

He turned from the dark, haunting beauty of the town and looked down at Laura. She blinked her eyes and drew her breath in sharply. She looked almost ugly, her face covered with sweat and grass stain. She was not like a girl. He wondered that he had never noticed before how anonymous was her gender, for this was the very central fact of her nature. She belonged nowhere, she fitted in no place at all, she had no home, no shell, no place of comfort or refuge, she was a fugitive with no place to run to. Others in her position might make some adjustment. The best of whatever is offered, however not right. But Laura would not accept it, none of the ways and means. The most imperfect part of her was the most pure. And that meant—

"Laura . . ." He held out his hand and put his heart in his eyes. She felt the sudden turning of understanding and took his hand and he pulled her gently to her feet.

For the first time they stood together in the dark without any fear

133

of each other, their hands loosely clasped and returning each other's look with sorrowful understanding, unable to help each other except through knowing, each completely separate and alone—but no longer strangers. . . .

SAWDUST

————◆⟨∞⟩◆————

Arthur Foff

"Sawdust" was published in STORY by an author unknown to us at the time. It came "over the transom," with no agent, friend, or teacher involved. In fact, the author, Arthur Foff, was a teacher himself at the University of Arizona. Later, he expanded "Sawdust" to novel length, and it was published as a STORY Press book, a novel, Glorious in Another Day.

As a short story, "Sawdust" has much in common with the William Faulkner story, "Barn Burning," discussed in chapter three. Dramatizing a similar boy–father relationship of painful inequality only partly understood by the boy, we are held by the same fearful anticipation of violence and suffering to come.

In both stories the basic conflict is acted out between two major characters—the father and the son; in this there is also a third, the pet dog. In each story, the father is shiftless, violent, and defeated; the boy is loving, sensitive, and hoping desperately that the act he fears will not take place, that the father he loves will resist the destructive forces within him. There is no ambivalence in the characters, or in the issues raised.

Other faces and voices and presences are brought in to give us further dimensions in understanding, but the focus never really leaves the two conflicting forces, as simple and as identifiable as good and evil.

I walked into Joe's and there was my old man at the bar as usual.
He was oiled pretty good and kept arguing with a skinny, yellow-
faced guy I figured I'd seen some place before.

"Pop," I said, "Maggie just had five pups, four males and a bitch,
why don't you come home and look them over?"

"Tom," Pop said, "you remember Mr. Finley here. He had Danny
Day." I remembered Finley now and I remembered Danny Day.
Danny Day had been a good dog. It had been about seven years ago
when I'd seen Danny's last fight. If you've maybe ever seen a sick
dog try and fight you know why it stuck in my mind though I was
only ten. Finley had lost a lot of good dogs besides Danny.

"Mr. Finley says he has a better dog than Danny ever was, a dog
that can whip anything I got. What do you think about that, Tom?"

"He maybe has, and he maybe hasn't. We're not fighting dogs any
more, what do we care?"

My pop turned back to the bar with his foot on the brass rail and
took a swallow of beer. He wiped his lips with his coat sleeve. "Sure,
I know we aren't going into the pit no more, O.K., but Mr. Finley
here says his Snatcher can lick anything I got. And I say he can't.
And I'm willing to bet my drawers even a pup like Moby Dick can
lick the hell out of him." I felt sick when he said that. I wanted to
get out of the bar and away from all the guys who hung around it.
I wanted to get back into the afternoon sunshine.

"You still talk a lot, like always." Finley spat into the spittoon.
"But I ain't interested in your talking. Three hundred bucks: put up
or shut up."

Pop turned back to the bar and pretended to drink his beer, but
I could see the roll of flesh on the back of his neck turn red. I said,
"How old is Moby? How old is he," I said.

"Two."

"Eighteen months."

"There isn't much difference," Pop said. He knew there was.

"Not much difference?" I stepped right up alongside him and
shook his arm. He wouldn't look at me, so I thought he was sore until

136

I saw his reflection in the mahogany mirror. It was a big mirror and his face seemed little in it, little and frightened and mad all at the same time. Then Joe, the bartender, moved in front of him and I couldn't see his face any more. Finley had been watching him, too, but now he turned and looked at me.

"Gentlemen," he said, staring hard, "you can't, you can't get good apples," he sneered at Pop, "off a bad tree."

The crowd laughed, even some of the racing men at the far end of the bar.

Pop faced Finley. He stood on his toes and shouted into Finley's face, "Damn you! We'll fight you and your crossbred cur!"

"The three hundred?" Finley acted like he wasn't interested. "Joe, bring another bottle."

"Don't worry about me, don't worry about me," Pop yelled in his ear, trying to pull him away from the bottle Joe had just set down in front of him.

Finley nodded. "Have a drink," he said.

A lot of guys had gathered around us and they were all talking at once, betting and swearing and asking when and where it was to be. Pop said would next month at the old pit outside Mill Valley be all right and Finley said any time, any place. Pop was bragging about what Moby would do to the Snatcher when I pushed through the circle of cigars, derbies, and fancy watch fobs to start home. Dick was my dog. He'd never been in a fight in his life.

The month passed like nothing. My old man didn't even bother to try and train Moby Dick. He stayed at Joe's all day, sometimes playing stud in back and sometimes standing at the bar with his beer. He talked about the fight whatever he was doing and there were big racing guys who hung onto everything he said, he told me, who'd never noticed him before. I tried to teach the dog a little myself, but he was my dog and I couldn't drive him and sweat him the way he needed. When Pop came home nights, which was usually late, he brought Moby into the parlor to pet him and talk to him. If he had a snoot full he'd feed him sausages on the sofa until he fell asleep. In the mornings he'd still be snoring on the sofa with his mouth open and Moby beside him.

When the first Thursday of the month rolled around, the time of the fight, I was shaky in my pants. The pit, which was in an old barn, had been fixed up by a half-brained Negro named George who'd been a good jockey until he got rheumatism. He'd made plenty of money for others but he didn't have any himself. He sold newspapers in front of Joe's now, bumming a drink when he could and doing errands for the guys who remembered him.

Pop and I took the ferry to Sausalito, driving the rest of the way to the old lumber barn outside Mill Valley. All the way over I rubbed Moby's head while Pop drove. "Moby," I'd say to him, "you'll win in no time, you're a cinch. You won't get a scratch and you'll win in no time." He'd wrinkle his nose up so his teeth showed in a smile because he liked to be talked to and have his head rubbed. He didn't know what I meant and I don't think I did myself. Whenever the car stopped suddenly he slobbered lightly but kept his cookies. That was lucky, I thought, it showed he wasn't too nervous.

We parked the car under some redwoods outside the barn and left Moby locked in it. After we'd opened up, a few guys drifted in, then more, and finally there was a big noisy crowd. I knew some of them and recalled others from when I'd been a kid. A couple of cops came in, but they were off duty. Pop shook hands with them and they said wasn't it just like the old days, and he said by God if it wasn't. Finley came in at eight-thirty on the dot just as Pop was walking around the inside of the pit inspecting it and cleaning his fingernails with his big jackknife, the way he does when he's worried.

Finley carried the Snatcher wrapped in a white towel through the crowd, set him in the pit, and took the towel off. It was the first time the Snatcher had been out to the coast and the crowd stopped talking to stare at him. He was an oversize brindle with a scar clean across the back of his head, and there were other marks from fighting on his chest and legs and muzzle. His chest was heavy as a beer keg; when he closed his mouth you could see the jaw muscles stand out like thick fists. Finley walked him around the pit twice to give the boys a chance to look him over and bet some more. Pop brought in Moby Dick and did the same. For a while you couldn't hear yourself think for the noise. New bets were placed. The odds went up in favor of the Snatcher to ten to one, but my old man kept putting down even money. Then at last it was quiet. Pop and Finley took the customary drink from the same bottle. The pup looked fine, you understand, but for all that he was a pup. He came from a good fighting line, only a fighting line don't mean a hell of a lot to a dog that hasn't ever been in a fight.

The dogs were placed opposite each other. The pit was closed. Pop leaned over the rail, talking low to Dick. The barn was almost black but for the yellow light dim in smoke over the pit. The sweet hard smell of whisky seemed everywhere. The crowd pressed to the rail. On the other side of the ring I could barely make out Finley's face, yellow as the light and blurred as the smoke. Moby stood with his head cocked at us. The Snatcher moved toward him and he stepped stiff and high away.

"Pop," I said, "look!"

Pop took a shot out of his bottle. "Don't worry, Tom," he said to me. "Moby'll lick the living hell out of him."

Just then the Snatcher flattened his small sharp trimmed ears and braced his hind legs in the sawdust. Moby was moving away when the Snatcher lunged. The hold missed but there was a nasty rip down Moby's shoulder. Right away he knew what it was about. His brown, pink-circled eyes became close and black and his lips curled back over his teeth in a snarl. He rumbled in his chest and braced his body until the muscles in his back quivered and bulged. The Snatcher moved in again and Dick met him with a hold for the throat that just missed. He struck again, fast and hard, for the same place. He missed. His teeth slid and tore along the base of the Snatcher's skull, reopening the scar and pouring blood down the Snatcher's neck. The Snatcher got his head away in a smooth rolling move that brought him right back. He slashed Moby's left ear into shreds, but missed the real hold he was trying for once more. The two of them backed away for a minute and for the first time I could see how the once white body of Dick was stained gold and red with sawdust and blood. Pop took another drink and swore under his breath. "God damn, God damn," he said. "God damn it, anyway."

The two snarls came at once. Moby moved too late. The Snatcher was on top of him. His teeth shone white for the second his mouth was open and then he fastened them in the lump of his shoulder muscle, forced his legs deeper into the sawdust so that he could sink the teeth to the bone. Once those teeth got there the bone would be smashed like a paper box.

"Roll, Moby, you damned fool, roll!" Pop finished the whisky in his bottle with a final gulp.

Instead of rolling away Moby tore away and the shoulder flesh tore wide open with him. He blurred in white, the flank of skin hanging like a flag, stained with blood and flecked with gold. I heard his jaws snap together once and miss, clean across the ring. I waited to hear the next empty smash. It didn't come.

I opened my eyes and saw he had the Snatcher solid by the throat. It must have been luck because he was a dog that didn't know enough to roll yet. The Snatcher tried uselessly to underslice at his gut. Moby held him away, threshing him back and forth, working in his hold. His thews jutted like rocks and the tendons in his legs got larger as they filled with blood from the strain. Slowly he began the slope of his shoulders to one side to bring the Snatcher down into the sawdust. For a minute the two dogs stood there, stuck in space, not moving and yet fighting with everything they had. Then the hump of muscle ridged across the Snatcher's shoulder line relaxed and Moby drove him to the ground. He worked the hold deeper and surer until the Snatcher could not even raise his head.

My old man raised the whisky bottle and cracked it over the rail. "Damn it, I told you. I told you he'd lick the hell out of him. I told you, didn't I?"

140

The Snatcher gave one last fine brave jerk to get away, then he settled back easy to the sawdust as if he'd decided to go to sleep. Finley, at the rail opposite, screwed his lips and spat cleanly into the ring onto the side of his dog's head where his eye was closed. He climbed the rail, walked across the pit without looking at the dogs, and stood in front of us. He said, "That was the luckiest hold I've seen in twenty years. A better dog wouldn't have even tried it."

"Lucky? Lucky?" Pop said, his voice getting louder. "A better dog? There ain't no better dog, nor no better line! See that Pit, see him out there? He wouldn't ever let loose his hold on the Snatcher's throat without you pry open his jaws. That's my kind of dog. He don't let loose!"

"Yeah?" said Finley, tilting back his hat.

One guy who had his arm around Pop's shoulder answered yeah, that dog couldn't take his teeth out of the Snatcher's throat if he wanted to. It was inside him to hold on. You could turn a fire hose on him and he wouldn't let go!

Everyone yelled and laughed. Sure, that was right. Moby Dick wouldn't give up his hold even if you turned a fire hose on him. Then, above all their voices, came my old man's. "A fire hose? Hell, you could cut his legs off and he wouldn't let go that throat hold!"

Finley took out his wallet and the barn became still. He looked at Pop, and Pop looked at him, and he said, "How much would you like to bet? Double or nothing?"

My old man stared at Finley, at me, at the faces of all the guys standing around him. Nobody said anything. A guy passed Pop a bottle and Pop took a big shot. The dim yellow light patched shadows on his face as he tilted his head back to drink and I could see the sweat oozing from the creases under his chin. He handed the bottle back and wiped his mouth with his sleeve. When he turned his head toward the pit everybody watched him. Moby was still holding fast. Then some wiseacre in the back yelled that he was yellow.

Pop wheeled around, clumsily, trying to keep his voice down.

"Double it is," he shouted. "Who wants another C?"

"I'll take that, pal." The voice was from the back again. Right away everyone went nuts.

"Another ten?"

"Hell, where's my dough?"

"Keep that damned cigar out of my face."

"Twenty-five'll get you fifty the dog gets loose. Here we go, boys. Who wants to take my easy money?"

"Hand me that bottle, you bastard."

"He won't go through with it, I tell you."

"Take this home to your whore. I told you to keep that cigar out of my face."

"Don't listen to them, Pop," I shouted. "Don't listen."

My old man looked at me once over his shoulder before the crowd surged forward, driving him toward the ring. He grabbed the rail. "Just a minute, just a minute," he yelled. "Who's going to do it?"

"It's your dog's legs," Finley said.

"It's impossible, impossible. He can't go through with it."

"That's right," shouted the wiseacre in the back, "he's yellow!"

Pop's face went hard. His chest rose and fell beneath his old brown sweater. Without a word he turned and climbed over the rail and walked across the pit to where Moby was holding onto the Snatcher.

"Don't, Pop," I screamed, "for the love of God, please don't!"

Some guy grabbed me and told me to shut up. He shoved me back and took my place at the rail. It seemed like everybody was shoving me. Pretty soon I was way in the back with nothing in front of me but heads. I clawed to the front again. It was too late. My old man was kneeling over the dogs so that his belly touched his knee. The light above him spilled yellow on his bald spot and gleamed in the sweat streaming off his cheeks.

The man next to me heaved when it was all over and he ran from the barn with his hand over his mouth. The whole place was wild with screaming. Two guys who'd bet Moby would hold on gave Pop another drink and helped him out of the pit. After he got out it didn't

142

seem as if he'd needed any help because he was talking and bragging the loudest of them all. "What'd I tell you? Licked the living—what do you think of the apple tree now, Finley? Here, here, who's got a drink? Yellow, boys, did you ever see the day I was yellow? Feel, feel? Feel a hundred percent, boys. Six hundred percent. Drinks on me at Joe's. No, no, didn't hurt him; only thinking about his hold— that's the way I breed them."

I just stood there and watched him go out with a big wad of greenbacks stuck in one fist and a bottle in the other. He went out and they went with him. Pretty soon I looked around and the barn was empty. Even the Negro George had left. There was nothing there but me and the two dogs and the yellow light.

I went into the pit and sat in the sawdust by Moby and the Snatcher: two good dogs, one of them mine, and both of them dead. I saw something shine on the ground. It was the jackknife, the blade still open. I shook off the blood, closed it, put it into my pocket.

I buried the two dogs under the redwoods in back of the barn. There were two trees close together. I buried Moby under the one, and the Snatcher under the other. The earth was soft and dark. I wanted to get into it too. I patted the last of the dirt into place with my hands because it seemed the thing to do.

It took me four hours to get to San Francisco. My old man had taken the car and I had to walk from the barn into Sausalito where I caught the last night ferry. When I walked into Joe's it was nearly morning and the stars were beginning to fade out of the sky. All the lights were on in Joe's and most of the guys were still there, laughing and patting Pop on the back, smoking cigars and drinking his whisky. I walked through the crowd. Pretty soon I came to him. I stood in back of him while the crowd gradually moved away until it was him and me there alone. "Pop," I said, "I want to talk to you." I maybe guess he'd seen me come toward him in the mahogany mirror because without turning he said, "Sure, sure, Tom." He yelled to his friends. "Hell, don't go away, boys. I'm standing them again soon's I put the kid in his place." He was very jolly. The guys began to move back to the bar.

I walked out the back door. Pop followed me. He shut the door and stood next to the big slop can with his back against the brick wall of the alley. I took the jackknife from my pocket. The alley was dirty and cold, with a mean wind blowing old papers down it that made scraping sounds. Above us the sky was purple and gray, lighted by the first streaks of the sun coming through the night clouds a golden red.

"Well," I said, "this isn't going to be as fine and courageous as cutting off your legs, but I maybe guess it'll have to do."

I put the point of the blade against his belly. There was a hole in the sweater where I put the knife. The threads had worn out and broke.

Pop didn't move. I looked up from the knife to his face, seeing the wetness on his cheeks.

"Best kid you ever seen," he said. He was smiling and the gold-red light of the sun was flush on his forehead. I closed the blade and handed him the jackknife. "It's yours," I said. I turned around and walked down the alley with the wind and the papers.

THE THIEF
ON THE CHAMPS ELYSEES

Hallie Burnett

I HAVE CHOSEN *one of my own stories because, in this first-person form, it has been technically interesting to me how a relatively minor episode can become so weighted with meanings in the fictional process. "The Thief on the Champs Élysées" appeared in my volume of short stories,* The Boarders in the Rue Madame, *and has been reprinted in magazines here and abroad, among them, interestingly enough,* Ellery Queen's Mystery Magazine.

Believing I was writing a literal account of an event which, disturbing as it was, I had experienced in a state of fascination with the developments, the characters, and my own initial panic, I found in the process of writing that this story somehow became the most fictional I had ever written. Even by peeling off the obvious layers of my own consciousness, so manifold and baffling in the end, I have never yet quite understood what it was trying to say.

I include it here because it seems to me an interesting and perhaps helpful example of how an idea around an actual experience may evolve into something else when one's "daemon is in charge"; when a writer has let herself "drift, wait, and obey," until an awareness not in her conscious mind comes to the surface of a story.

Standing before the kiosk waiting for a copy of *l'Express*, I suddenly felt my big leather handbag weightless as an empty pillowcase, and I did not have to look inside to know I had been robbed by the girl in the *Prisunic*.

My first impulse was to cry out to the gendarme standing like a giant gull flapping his cape wings at the turbulent six o'clock traffic from his island on the Champs Élysées. But by the time I had taken a step forward he had blown his whistle at a stalled motorist and had begun to shout such invective that, naturally, I reconsidered. A man too deep in any rôle does not care to be interrupted; it was doubtful, anyway, if he would consider a petty crime in a French five-and-dime store of any great importance.

There was a second, younger gendarme watching like an understudy from a window of a stationary police car, but seeing his concentration, I knew that to neither of them could I give way to hysteria. So I turned back to the kiosk, handed over the one franc for my newspapers (leaving only four new francs in my change purse), then spent another twenty-five centimes for *Le Figaro*. But my poise vanished at the moment this last coin left my hand and I raced back to the corner entrance of the *Prisunic*.

The doorway now was blocked by two dogs and a crowd of shoppers hilariously observing the somewhat distracted attempts of a large proletarian mongrel and a small, aristocratic white poodle to mate. It was only when the mongrel was dragged away by the nervous lad who was his master that the mistress of the elegant poodle managed to restrain her little bitch; but still the public remained to laugh and discuss *l'affaire* with the poodle's mistress, a cunningly designed bitch herself, in white wool and pink makeup.

"Naughty, naughty," she cried, and wagged her own white derriere in unison with her pet's as though she herself had felt the challenge of the attack.

"Excuse, please. *Excusez-moi!*" I pleaded, pushing against the crowd. Resentfully they let me through, their faces plainly saying,

146

Here is another American tourist possessed of not a shred of feeling for the most amusing facts of life.

As it was only by pushing and struggling that I got through to the counter where, the moment before, I had been trying on a cheap, ridiculous hat, I refused to be intimidated by the crowd. Yet the *vendeuse*, once I had attracted her attention, stared as though she had never seen me, and for a moment this took all courage from me.

"Didn't you see the German girl?" I cried, breaking in on another customer. "The one beside me a moment ago? When I tried on these hats? Did you see her leave? Do you know which way she went?" I speak an American French, it is true, but surely she understood.

Handing a straw cloche to the customer, she retorted: "*Je ne comprends pas!*" I am ordinarily a coward before antagonism and I trembled, but did not retreat.

"I no understan'," the German girl had said to me in English— but that was before she had asked, "You do not find a hat you like?" with so little accent that I thought she was a fellow American presuming on our nationality; also I had not cared for the way she was crowding up against me. Then I turned and saw the foreign look. Although her soiled blond hair was cut in the same style as mine, it was clinging moistly to a broad square forehead; and, while the skin was young, it was marred by imperfections, as though she did not eat regularly or well. Yet there was also a familiarity about the face which puzzled me. Had I perhaps seen her at the École Française (she had seemed to know me by sight), or did she resemble some person I had known in the past?

I recalled that a traveling American must be friendly with all strangers, so I managed a distant but polite smile, at the same time drawing away from the touch of the girl's heavy coat against my bare arm (after all, it was a warm day in early September).

"The head sizes are too small for me," I replied, an admission which sometimes sounds boastful but always makes me think a cow's head is larger than a monkey's.

The girl disappeared, but, to my surprise, she reappeared at my right side. And she looked at me coldly then as though she'd not been the one to speak first and could not now imagine why I spoke to her at all!

"I no understan'," she said, with such a marked, guttural accent I wondered if I had been mistaken, if it had been someone else who had spoken before. And then the next instant, like a whitecapped wave dissolved by the swell of the sea, the girl vanished into the crowd, having by then extracted my passport folder from the handbag over my left arm.

"I've been robbed," I tried to say calmly to the saleswoman. I leaned across the counter to bring my words closer and clearer to her, for I could not allow her to ignore me. "The girl who stood here a moment ago—You saw her! You spoke to her and to me."

The *vendeuse* shrugged and coolly turned to rearrange her hats on the shelves as though the subject were closed—as though the girl I had spoken of, so far as she remembered this day or any other, had never existed.

Nervous tears rose in my eyes and turning quickly I knocked my frail paper bag, filled with objects I'd bought, against the counter, where it broke. (So many things which should be strong in France are frail, like paper bags, and things thought to be weak are granite, like this woman.) My small gifts for friends scattered like hailstones, the cans of goose liver and pork pâté, the glass beads, pink soap, scarves, and perfume bottles with flower-trimmed necks, rolled, cluttered, fluttered or crashed into the aisle, and one passing Frenchwoman was hit on the foot by a perfume vial in the shape of a pig. I stopped to retrieve the nearest articles, thrusting these into my empty handbag (where my passport folder had been the hour before), then retreated into the crowd to lean against a counter where the red, blue, green and yellow hats whirled into a spectrum of undistinguishable colors before my eyes.

I had not gone back to my French class on the Left Bank that afternoon after the fitting of my Chantilly lace dress at Mlle. Boucicault's on the Boulevard Haussmann because I felt too elevated by my glorified appearance in the dark mirror to settle down to another daily battle of French verbs in company with other accents as bad as my own. There, in the dim room where the little seamstress strained her eyes, I had seen myself as I could be: my square brow almost distinguished-looking, my dark blond hair Rapunzelian, and my full face luminous as a photograph of the Princess d'X in the last issue of *Réalités*; so I rebelled. However, like many rebels, I had no cause, so the best thing I could think of was to go to a movie on the Champs Élysées.

Then, since the black lace gown was costing me twenty dollars more than I'd put aside for it, I passed up a film I wanted to see for a grade-B picture made for French consumption only (there being a difference of four new francs between the two), and the dialogue in this was incomprehensible, the plot confused and the setting regional. I had walked out before the end with still an hour of freedom before I was expected back at the Pension for the evening meal, when I noticed the *Prisunic* doors were open and I decided this was an unexpected opportunity to purchase small gifts to take back home.

My loose change was quickly gone, and it was necessary to take out the passport folder where I kept large bills—with my American Express checks, my SAS plane ticket, vaccination certificate and other personal papers. Unfortunately, in order to remove one ten-franc note, I had to expose all, including the green end of my American passport; and while this had never bothered me before that moment, I felt a curious sense of impending danger.

I could not reasonably explain this, nor can I now, yet it was as though some magnetic force were drawing that folder from my hands; and the sensation was so physical and so intense that after I had replaced the folder my arm actually ached. I recall rubbing my shoulder in alarm as though the strain had drawn heavily on the muscles of my heart, and then, as now, it seemed that I might faint. . . .

Now again, a weakness came over me, and I fell into that pit of clairvoyance where the sense of danger is as staggering as a drop from a precipice in a dream. So I understood quite clearly that by the time I'd put my folder out of sight it had already, in effect, been stolen by a thief in the *Prisunic*.

The weakness passed and anger returned as I opened my eyes on the increasing disorder of the milling French crowd with the dinner hour beginning to stir their bellies and their temper. My impulse was now to get away, let it go, make out the best I could; but I thought if only someone would help me, I might still be able to find the German girl and force her to return my passport folder. After all, I was in a bad way without it.

"Where does one find the manager?" I asked another saleswoman, politely, but since she was concluding a sale and I had made her lose count of the change, she too stared in resentment. Then someone directed me to a long white basement passageway in the rear, and, turning my back upon the crowd, I entered upon a stretch of white walls and utter, unexpected silence in a passageway that must have tunneled far back under a city block.

Here was no visible exit other than the way I had come (the three doors I passed, running down the corridor, seemed closed and locked forever), but at the far end where I made a turn to the left I found a heavy door bolted like a vault. There was a smell of dryness now as from a well-stoked furnace and it seemed to me this might have been a gas chamber in the days of the Nazi Occupation; certainly I had been misdirected, so I turned and ran quickly back, down the white hall until, seeing one of the three doors open, I paused and looked inside to meet the eyes of a man standing over a white porcelain urinal. For one awful instant we both stared, unable to break the lock of mutual horror, then I fled through the door and out into the street.

The gendarme in the police car now was facing the other way, dreaming over orange umbrellas spread open like exotic fruits above the green tables of a café, but as I ran toward him his eyes turned and examined me with mild interest.

"A thief! *Une voleuse!*" I cried, before I again lost my nerve. "*Monsieur, s'il vous plaît*—I have been robbed in the *Prisunic!*"

He jumped out of his car at once, spoke rapidly to the officer on the safety island, and then entered the store with me. There he asked questions to right and to left so imperiously that in spite of the same blank stares as before, I was charmed and encouraged by his authority. And the hat saleswoman, this time, was not so indifferent, even though she still denied having seen anyone beside me at the counter in the past hour. There had been only one *étrangère*, she insisted, since noon: this one (who was I).

Like searching for a pebble on a rocky shore when the tide has come and gone, we wandered from counter to counter until the female manager appeared from the depths to pronounce any theft here *impossible*. If Mam'selle would only produce the proof, she said, or perhaps if I looked again in my bag, I would find the object which I thought I had lost.

"I did not lose anything," I said, firmly. "My passport folder with my identification, my money, everything I own, was stolen in this store. I only wish help in finding the German girl who stood beside me." I pointed out the saleswoman. "It seems very strange that *she* will not admit this."

The manager continued to shake her head as other customers gathered around, and some were friendly to me, a stranger in trouble, and some were not, seeing I was American. But the young gendarme stood steady and unflinching as a rock, coming back again and again with his sharp, hard questions; then we were again on the street, the store closing for the night, and nothing had been accomplished.

I waited beside my defender as he consulted a new, small book. "*Le Commissariat.* Ah," he murmured, his finger moving down the pages, then all at once I understood he must be very new in the

151

service, or he would not be so eager to help, and so uninformed. His uniform too was fresh, new, unwrinkled, his shoes and belt highly polished (doubtless even his gun was still untried!); then, as I watched, his hard round chin puckered, his Norman blue eyes brightened, and even his tan mustache lifted with a charming smile.

Moistening his red lips, he showed me what he had been looking for in the book. "We go there!" he said, and we set off together on the rue Balzac where he made a sharp left into the rue Lord Byron, and then a sharp right, like an excited school boy in search of a darting squirrel. Tonight he would no doubt return to his parents (I decided he was too young and thoughtless for wife and child) who would listen to his prattle about an American woman who had carried in her handbag as much money as a Frenchman spends in a year for his wine; and then I caught the eye of a passer-by and understood that I myself could seem to be a criminal, dragged along by the police! Once again I had the impulse to bolt, but by then it was too late. Unexpectedly my gendarme asked, with some concern, "*Ça va bien?*" And my face must surely have been a mess, red and soiled, with my hair hanging limp as the German thief's across her forehead.

"*Ça va,*" I returned crossly, but then he moved to the outer edge of the walk and motioned me on ahead, apparently deciding at last that it was safe to be more agreeable. After that we walked along as equals, talking of this thing that had happened to me, he even understanding my French, and I—since he spoke with peasant slowness—understanding his. The accidental meeting of our eyes was so agreeable that by the time we reached the Commissariat on the Faubourg-du-Roule in the 8th Arrondissement we were remarkably at ease with one another, so that my protector introduced me to the elder of the two officers as tenderly as though we had been in love.

A small Algerian standing before the court tapped lightly and respectfully on the counter. "*Je vous en prie, Monsieur le Commissaire.* We stand here first. Hear me, please," he requested, and his sullen woman twisted a finger through a black curl, narrowing her eyes at me. But the officials were more interested in my case and spoke in such a way that the poor couple moved back to a bench against the wall with the resignation of those who must always wait on official favor.

Now, with gallantry, my gendarme began our story, and I was pleased that he told it so well, encouraged by his superiors who listened like elders sponsoring a young man and are delighted at his making good. The second official, however, had to leave for his dinner and rose, shaking hands with his colleague, nodding approvingly and encouragingly at the gendarme, and at the door his eyes lingered a moment upon my legs and this also seemed friendly and human. Then we got down to the business of the theft.

The Commissaire stated his passionate regret that I, an American guest of Paris, had been treated so badly. That I, a lovely lady, must understand that Paris was really not a lawless city—not like New York, which our own Mayor, interviewed last week by *France-Soir*, had admitted to be shockingly full of unsolved crimes.

At this moment a small and humble detective came in on my case, with a dog nervy and tail-wagging as any stray along a country road, and although one could hardly take either of them seriously, the dog's tongue dripped with anticipation, his eyes glistened, and he pulled on the leash as though eager to get on with the chase. I could not understand why they returned back through the door through which they had come—which could not possibly lead to the *Prisunic*—since I had been requested to give the dog a friendly sniff of my hand which held the bag.

I did not wish, however, to criticize Monsieur le Commissaire, who was certainly doing his best. Even now he was writing out a report for the American Embassy, a favor I had not thought of asking.

"They will be *très, très agités,*" he said. "A passport is taken seriously by your Government, Madame. And by ours," he added hastily.

Then he asked if I had enough francs for my dinner, putting his hand in his pocket, and I was touched by this, but explained that I

153

was perhaps still expected at my Pension, late as it was. At that he himself telephoned Mlle. du Coeur, conversing with her in the polished manner she prefers, and when he bowed me away at last it seemed as though we had met in social surroundings and only incidentally were in these drab police headquarters which, now that I thought about it, had the smell of frightful but detected crimes.

At the last moment my eyes met those of my gendarme (whose name I never knew!), seeing his expression so regretful, his red lips so moist and his eyes so soft and brooding that it seemed something profoundly emotional had been shared between us in this most exceptional hour of our intimacy. He even took a step toward me, impulsively, as a lover, wishing to keep me from leaving—but it was too fragile a thing between us, and the older man, sympathetically but firmly, reached out and put a restraining hand upon his arm.

As I passed the Algerian couple stirring hopefully on their bench, I felt quite misty-eyed, and it was not until I found myself again on the darkening street, the lamps now lighted, that I remembered the thief herself had not, after my first description, been referred to by anyone again.

Back at the Pension I was greeted with excitement, and there was a small supper which Mlle. du Coeur had placed in my room, ham and cheese and an orange from Spain, with my own bottle of cold white wine, a clean napkin wrapped about its neck. So when I went to bed at last I felt comforted as a child after a storm of tears. It was not until much later, in my dreams, I found the German girl beside me once more, somehow increasingly familiar, the same height as myself, although she had seemed less tall the hours before. And my sense of well-being vanished, so that I wept, awakening with a sense of loss more personal and disturbing than any I had ever known.

Lightheartedness briefly returned next day when the Scandinavian Airlines gave me another ticket, and a Frenchman at the American

Express office issued new traveler's checks to me equal in value to those stolen with my passport.

"We may ask you later to identify any forgeries," he said, and I begged to be allowed to do this, to do anything to show my gratitude. I also suggested that the checks be particularly watched for in Germany, since the thief had spoken with a German accent.

"Would you give me a brief description?" he asked, although I thought I had done this.

"She was about my height," I said, "and also my coloring. It is even possible that if we dressed alike she might somehow resemble me." This I said on the impulse of the moment, for it had not occurred to me before. I could not understand why the young man seemed startled at what I said.

Then at the American Consulate I discovered the precarious balance of my situation, for I failed to be received with any friendliness at all.

"A lost passport," said the narrow-chinned, pale-lipped woman official, "places the guilt squarely upon the loser, Mrs. Greenhill."

"But I did not lose it! Here is the report of the Commissioner of Police," I said, thrusting the document across her desk. "This is the proof if there is any doubt in your mind."

But the woman only looked at me with further dislike and touched the tip of a pointed tongue to her upper lip, shaking her head. "This only says that you reported your passport stolen: I fail to see any *proof*. I can only repeat, an American passport is not a thing to be treated lightly."

"I went to the police—and they believed me!" But I saw then I was being accused of something.

"Those Frenchmen can be fooled," she said, briefly. "We cannot."

"I have my reservation to go home on Friday," I said, fighting for control. "I must have a passport—I cannot possibly stay in Paris any longer!"

"We are not a welfare agency," said the woman, coldly.

"Everyone has been helpful," I protested. "Even the Commissioner of Police offered to lend me francs for my dinner." Yet when I saw the nasty look on her face I knew I had been foolish to say this.

"I doubt that an officer of the French Government would lend money to any woman—except at a price!" she said dryly, and I saw we were fighting the most primitive battle of all, the generosity of men toward one kind of woman and not to another.

"If I don't have my passport by Friday, I will lose my reservation and—perhaps more," I said quietly. I could not tell her I was going home to be remarried to a man I had divorced, and that I could not now bear to wait another hour. She would have no more sympathy for that kind of nonsense than for any other. "Please—surely there is something you can do."

So, finally, perhaps trapped by my false humility, the woman stared with resentful eyes and told me to return on Wednesday. "With photos, and accompanied by someone to identify you. In the meantime—try to find your passport."

On Wednesday I went back with three photos and an acquaintance from the Pension who carried driver's license, insurance papers, personal mail and an American library card: but, alas, she had forgotten to bring her own passport, which was in her husband's coat pocket. The assistant consul became quite cheery when she discovered this and sent me away again empty-handed, saying to come back on Thursday.

But Thursday turned out to be a holiday, which I had not foreseen, nor, perhaps, had she. So the acquaintance and I, who had hurried through breakfast in order to appear at nine-thirty, were turned away again. There had been rain in the night, and when we saw it still looked threatening, the lady from the Pension decided to go right back to her room. I found a small café a block from the Consulate and sat there over coffee, brooding. Who and what I was if I had been asked to prove my existence at that moment, I did not know, for it seemed one could not exist without papers and the official approval of the baleful, cold-natured assistant lady consular employee. But the thief, I thought suddenly, the German girl, how easy it must be now for her! All she has to say is: Here is *my* passport, *my* money, *my* checks, and she will be honored, while I, who can be identified only by my face, my bones and my speech, am unaccepted, accused of not telling the truth.

But the thought of that girl intrigued me. Perhaps she has a lover, I thought, a Frenchman; and since Friday at six P.M. they must have spent many of those crisp decorative, new ten-franc notes. The girl also, surely, will have bought a new, lighter coat and had her blond hair washed. And if her lover *is* a Frenchman they will also have eaten good food and drunk fine wines, which even so soon as this may have improved the texture of her skin.

Yet I barely had money for this extra coffee, and the lace dress would have to be cancelled, that pale, transfigured face rising from the mirror of Mlle. Boucicault forgotten as though it had never been.

Feeling intense self-pity, seeing again that mirror which now reflected no image of myself at all, I was relieved when an American Army man I'd met the week before came by and sat down beside me. Listening to my unhappy story he, being a man of action, at once took charge. Even though it was a holiday, he got up from the table and telephoned a friend in the Embassy and stormed about my treatment, saying if something was not done *toute suite*, he'd raise holy hell! If they gave me a runaround this time, I heard him say, "By God, we'll move in with the Army!"

Thus the next morning I was received quickly by the assistant lady consul, and although she found one last way of annoying me (my pictures were not acceptable and I must go to a photographer down the street who charged three times the ordinary fee), I stood before her at last, complete with all requirements. She looked at my witness's documents, she looked at the forms I had filled in, and she looked at my newest photo.

"This doesn't look like you," she complained, but now only as someone forced to accept irritating reality. And certainly the photo did not: with that harassed look on my face and my neglected blond hair, I resembled more the German thief than I did myself!

Yet I managed to keep my tongue, even when she gave me a passport good for only six days, although I was laughing hysterically when I went, for the last time, out the Consulate door.

Back in New York at last, I remained grateful to the French gendarme and the Commissaire, to Mlle. du Coeur, the Frenchman at the American Express and to the Major of the American Army. I told the story several times about the unkindness of the American consul's assistant, and friends said I should write to my congressman or to the newspapers, which I never did. I was remarried and happy, and was glad to put the whole thing from my mind. Until one morning four months later, when a letter came from a Mr. Brown at the Express Company asking me to call and identify signatures on checks I had reported lost in Paris.

Feeling oddly relieved that here at last was proof that I had been robbed, I telephoned and said I would be delighted to come down, although I hadn't really thought the checks would ever be returned.

"Why not?" Mr. Brown asked. I did not know, I said, although I supposed it was because of the German girl.

"Were you in Germany then, Mrs. Greenhill? I understood you were only in France."

This seemed irrelevant, but I explained it was a German girl who had stolen them from my handbag in the *Prisunic.*

"I did not know that," he said. Somewhat hastily, I said I would be right down.

I was delayed by various duties so that it was three hours before I ascended the old-fashioned elevator and entered a room which seemed the sum total of all official rooms in the world. I'd been in quite a number since I'd started this search for my possessions, the police station in the Faubourg-du-Roule, the Express office in Paris, the Consulate—all cheerless, repelling blocks of granite challenge to unproven claims of humanity.

"I'm expected," I said to the girl at the switchboard, and a young man stood halfway down that big room and motioned to me. His face was reassuringly young, although blank and smooth, and expressionless eyes gave me a searching look of inspection before we sat down. Then he opened a folder on his desk and placed it on my lap.

"There are the checks, Mrs. Greenhill," he said. "Please examine them carefully. Tell me, if you can, which signatures are real and which are fraudulent."

"Zurich!" I exclaimed. "They speak German there—at least I was not wrong about the girl's accent."

"All our checks are cleared through Zurich," he informed me, as though I had said something stupid. "Now, the signatures—please."

There was my name at the top of each check as I had signed it in my own bank and there was the counter-signature in the lower right-hand corner, also in my handwriting—small, impatient, too rapid for style, and too slanting, I have been told, for emotional stability. And all of these signatures, there was no doubt about it, must be mine.

"They look all right," I said, thinking this was some trick to show me only my own signed checks; then I counted them, and saw there were far too many here for that.

"Please look again, Mrs. Greenhill. This is a very serious matter."

I picked up the checks one by one, examining each letter, becoming so absorbed that I did not at once notice a woman who joined us. But when I looked up to say that it was still absurdly difficult to swear I had not written them all, she was looking over his shoulder with the same bright, observant, accusing smile I'd last seen on the face of the woman assistant consul in Paris.

It was important that they understand, so I began to tell them all the circumstances of the theft. This thief on the Champs Élysées who had been so clever as to master my signature was a dull-looking creature as she'd stood beside me in the *Prisunic*, I said. So how could they explain this thing the German girl had done—mastering an imitation of my handwriting which had been shaped by my own three hundred years of American environment? Were there no national differences anymore? I went distractedly on, about the girl and me at opposite poles, and how she had stood there trying on a hat and watching me—but the *vendeuse* had claimed she remembered only one of us.

"Mrs. Greenhill, will you please, once more, describe this girl."

"Yes, of course." But suddenly I faltered, my face grew hot and I found myself snapping the catch on my small city handbag. And although I needed a cigarette, I dared not reach for one, knowing that my hand would tremble. For the truth was now that I could not remember the face of the girl nor evoke her in my mind. Even as I tried to say the words I thought I had said before—blond, my height, a wide, square forehead, round flushed face, brown eyes—it seemed I was describing not a stranger, but myself!

Then again it was as it had been in the *Prisunic,* when I was fighting for possession against a will strong enough to draw my life's blood, challenging my own right to keep what was privately and exclusively my own. Now again, it seemed I was protecting something perhaps less tangible but of even greater value: my own belief in myself. "The man at the Express office in Paris believed me, you know," I said, wretchedly, seeing plainly enough what they all were thinking. "*He* did not once suggest I might have lost it—"

"Nor have we," said Mr. Brown, exchanging glances with the woman. "Even though there have been no other thefts reported in that district for a year."

"A year ago," said the woman, "a Frenchwoman with a red purse did a job in that store. Yet it is hard to see how a German girl could have escaped without attracting more attention."

There is no German girl, they seemed to say, where is your proof? Here are the checks you reported lost and the others the foolish Frenchman in our office gave you—but the signatures, you see, are all the same.

Then unexpectedly Mr. Brown leaned forward and touched one finger to the smaller pile of checks. "Those are the forgeries, Mrs. Greenhill. You will observe the movement of the pen on the final letters, and how the 'r' is not the same. So there is nothing more we need ask of you at this moment—although since two are still missing we may call on you again. Thank you for coming in."

The trial was ended, and they meant for me to go. But this was not fair; I could see even then that they had not taken my word for all this, and I wanted to prove it to them, and to the gendarme and the Commissaire who had looked so sad to have me leave—for they had not believed me, either: I understood that at last. I was the only one who had seen the German girl, who could not now be properly described, yet she was still abroad in the world, still uncommitted and still free   my deadliest enemy, who had stolen my money, my passport, and my face.

INDIAN SUMMER

Erskine Caldwell

THIS RITES-OF-PASSAGE story is one nearly all good writers have tackled from time to time, and should. Awakening sexuality, in the young male, with its confusions, half-cruelties, and reluctant tenderness, provides us with a perfect means of examining what the short story is all about: a revealing moment, out of time, in the lives of characters for whom we must be made to care. Like love itself, it is unpredictable, yet deeply familiar.

The author, whose amazing versatility in writing covers journalism, playwriting (Tobacco Road will never be forgotten!), novels, and short stories, writes that "Indian Summer" is one story he has remained fond of through the years.

The water was up again. It had been raining for almost two whole days, and the creek was full to the banks. Dawn had broken gray that morning, and for the first time that week the sky was blue and warm.

Les pulled off his shirt and unbuckled his pants. Les never had to bother with underwear, because as soon as it was warm enough in the spring to go barefooted he hid his union suit in a closet and left it there until fall. His mother was not alive, and his father never bothered about the underclothes.

"I wish we had a shovel to dig out some of the muck," he said. "Every time it rains this hole fills up with this stuff. I'd go home and get a shovel, but if they saw me they'd make me stay there and do something."

While Les was hanging his shirt and pants on a bush, I waded out into the yellow water. The muck on the bottom was ankle deep, and there were hundreds of dead limbs stuck in it. I pulled out some of the largest and threw them on the other bank out of the way.

"How's the water, Jack?" Les asked. "How deep is it this time?"

I waded out to the middle of the creek where the current was the strongest. The yellow water came almost up to my shoulders.

"Nearly neck deep," I said. "But there's about a million dead limbs stuck in the bottom. Hurry up and help me throw them out."

Les came splashing in. The muddy water gurgled and sucked around his waist.

"I'll bet somebody comes down here every day and pitches these dead limbs in here," Les said, making a face. "I don't see how else they could get here. Dead tree limbs don't fall into a creek this fast. Somebody is throwing them in, and I'll bet a pretty he doesn't live a million miles away, either."

"Maybe Old Howes does it, Les."

"Sure, he does it. He's the one I'm talking about. I'll bet anything he comes down and throws limbs in every day."

Les stepped on a sharp limb. He held his nose and squeezed his eyes and ducked under and pulled it out.

"You know what?" Les said.

"What?"

"Old Howes told Pa we scared his cows last Saturday. He said we made them run so much he couldn't get them to let down their milk Saturday night."

"This creek bottom isn't his. Old Howes doesn't own anything down here except that pasture on the other side of the fence. We haven't even been on the other side of the fence this year, have we?"

"I haven't seen Old Howes' cows all summer. If I did see them,

I wouldn't run them. He just told Pa that because he doesn't want us to come swimming in the creek."

Pieces of dead bark and curled chips suddenly came floating down the creek. Somewhere up there the trash had broken loose from a limb or something across the water. I held my arms V-shaped and caught the bark and chips and threw them out of the way.

Les said something, diving down to pull up a dead limb. The muck on the bottom of the creek was so deep we could not take a step without first pulling our feet out of the sticky mud; otherwise we would have fallen flat on our faces in the water. The muck had a stink like a pig pen.

Les threw the big limb out of sight.

"If Old Howes ever comes down while we're here and tells us to get out of the creek, let's throw muck at him. Are you game, Jack? Wouldn't you like to do that to him just once?"

"That's what we ought to do to him, but we'd better not, Les. He would go straight and tell my folks, and your Pa."

"I'm not scared of Old Howes," Les said, making a face. "He hasn't got me buffaloed. He wouldn't do anything. He's scared to tell anybody. He knows we'd catch him sometime and mud-cake him."

"I don't know," I said. "He told on me that time I caught his drake and put it in that chicken run of his."

"That was a long time—" Les stopped and listened.

Somebody had stepped on a dead limb behind the bushes. The crack of the wood was loud enough to be heard above the splashing and gurgling in the creek.

"What's that?" both of us said.

"Who's that?" Les asked me.

"Listen!" I said. "Duck down and be quiet."

Behind the bushes we could hear someone walking on dead twigs and dry leaves. Both of us squatted down in the water until only our heads were above it.

"Who is it?" Les whispered to me.

I shook my head, holding my nose under the water.

164

The yellow water swirled and gurgled through the tree roots beside us. The roots had been washed free of earth by the high waters many years before, and now they were old-looking and covered with bark.

Les squatted lower and lower until only his eyes and the top of his head were showing. He held his nose under the water with both hands. The water was high, and its swiftness and muddy-heaviness made gurgling sounds that echoed up and down the creek.

Suddenly the bushes parted, and Jenny came through. When Les saw her, his eyes popped open and he jerked his head above the water to get his breath. The noise he made when the water bubbled scared all three of us for a moment.

Jenny was Old Howes' daughter. She was about our age, possibly a year or two older.

Les saw her looking at our clothes hanging on the bushes. He nudged me with his elbow.

"What are you doing down here?" Les said gruffly, trying to scare her.

"Can't I come if I want to?"

"You can't come down here when we're in swimming. You're not a boy."

"I can come if I wish to, smarty," Jenny said. "This creek doesn't belong to you."

"It doesn't belong to you, either," Les said, making a face. "What are you going to do about that?"

"All right," Jenny said, "if you are going to be so mean about it, Leslie Blake, I'll take your clothes and hide them where you'll never find them again as long as you live. What are you going to do about that?"

Jenny reached for the clothes. She grabbed Les's pants and my shirt and union suit.

Les caught my arm and pulled me toward the bank. We couldn't hurry at first, because we had to jerk our feet out of the muck before we could move at all.

"Let's duck her, Jack," Les whispered. "Let's give her a good ducking. Come on."

We crawled up the bank and caught Jenny just as she was starting to run through the bushes with our clothes. Les locked his arms around her waist and I caught her arms and pulled as hard as I could.

"I'll scream!" Jenny said. "If you don't stop, I'll scream at the top of my lungs. Papa is in the pasture, and he'll come right away. You know what he'll do to both of you, don't you?"

"We're not afraid of anybody," Les said, scowling and trying to scare her.

I put my hand over her mouth and held her with one arm locked around her neck. Together we pulled and dragged her back to the bank beside the creek.

"Don't you want to duck her, Jack?" Les said. "Don't you think we ought to? She's been telling Old Howes tales about us. She's a tattletale tit."

"We ought to duck her, all right," I said. "But suppose she goes and tells on us about that?"

"When we get through ducking her, she won't tell any more tales on us. We'll duck her until she promises and crosses her heart never to tell anybody. She's the one who's been throwing dead limbs into the creek every day. I'll bet anything she's the one who's been doing it."

Jenny was helpless while we held her. Les had her around the waist with both arms, and I still held her neck locked in the crook of my left arm. She tried to bite my hand over her mouth, but every time she tried to hurt me, I squeezed her neck so hard she had to stop.

I was a little afraid to duck Jenny, because once we had ducked a colored boy named Bisco, and it had almost drowned him. We ducked Bisco so many times he couldn't breathe, and he became limp all over. We had to stretch him out on the ground and roll him over and over, and all the time we were doing that, yellow creek water was running out of his mouth. I was afraid we might drown Jenny. I didn't know what would happen to us if we did that.

"I know what let's do to her, Les," I said.

"What?"

"Let's mud-cake her."

"What's the matter with ducking her? It will scare her and make her stop throwing dead limbs into the creek. It'll stop her from telling tales about us, too."

"We'd better not duck her, Les," I said. "Remember the time we ducked Bisco? We nearly drowned him. I don't want anything like that to happen again."

Les thought a while, looking at Jenny's back. She was kicking and scratching all the time, but she couldn't begin to hurt us, and we had her so she couldn't get loose.

"All right," Les said. "We'll mud-cake her then. That's just as good as ducking, and it'll teach her a lesson. It'll make her stop being a tattletale tit."

"She's going to tell on us anyway, so we'd better do a good job of it this time. But it ought to make her stop throwing dead limbs into the swimming hole, anyway."

"She won't tell on us after we get through with her," Les said. "She won't tell anybody. She won't even tell Old Howes. Ducking and mud-caking always stops kids from telling tales. It's the only way to cure it."

"All right," I said, "let's do it to her. She needs ducking, or mud-caking, or something. Somebody has got to do it to her, and we're the right ones to make a good job of it. I'll bet she won't bother us again after we get through with her."

Les threw Jenny on the ground beside the bank, locking her arms behind her back and holding her face in the earth so she couldn't make any noise. Les had to straddle her neck to keep her still.

"Take off her clothes, Jack," Les said. "I've got her. She can't get away as long as I'm holding her."

I reached down to pull off her dress, and she kicked me full in the stomach with both feet. When I fell backward and tried to sit up, there was no breath left in me. I opened my mouth and tried to yell at Les, but I couldn't even whisper.

"What's the matter, Jack?" Les said, turning his head and looking at me.

I got up on both knees and doubled over, holding my stomach with both arms.

"What's the matter with you, Jack?" he said. "Did she kick you?"

Les's back had been turned and he had not seen what Jenny had done to me.

"Did she kick me!" I said weakly. "It must have been her, but it felt like a mule. She knocked all of the wind out of me."

"Sit on her legs, then," Les said. "She can't kick you if you do that."

I ran down to the side of the creek and came back with a double handful of yellow muck. When I dug it out of the creek, it had made a sucking sound, and the odor was worse than any that ever came out of a pig pen. The muck in the creek stank worse than anything I had ever smelled. It was nothing but rotted leaves and mud, but it smelled like decayed eggs and a lot of other things.

I got Jenny's dress off and tossed it on the bushes so it would not get covered with muck. Les was able to hold her arms and cover her mouth at the same time by then, because she was not nearly so strong as either of us.

"She's got underwear on, Les," I said.

"Sure she has," Les said. "All girls wear underclothes. That's what makes them so sissy."

"You're not talking about me, are you?" I said, looking at him. "Because if you are—"

"I'm talking about her," Les said. "I know you have to wear the stuff because your people make you do it. But girls like to have it on. They don't want to go without it. That's why girls are so sissy."

"All right," I said, "but don't try to get nasty with me, because I'll—"

"You won't do anything, so shut up. Hurry and take her clothes off."

168

"Are we going to strip her naked?" I said.

"Sure," Les said. "We've got to. We can't mud-cake her if we don't strip her, can we?"

"I know that," I said, "but suppose Old Howes came down and saw us—"

"Old Howes wouldn't do nothing but spit and slip up in it. Who's scared of him anyway? I'm not."

After we had struggled with Jenny a while longer, and after her underclothes were finally off, Les said he was tired of holding her. He was puffing and blowing as if he had been running five miles without stopping to rest.

I took Jenny's arms and put my hand over her mouth and sat on her neck. Les picked up a big handful of muck and threw it at her. The muck struck her on the stomach, making a sound like slapping water with a plank. He threw another handful. It splattered all over us.

While Les was running to the creek for another load, I turned Jenny over so he could smear some on her back. She did not struggle anymore now, but I was afraid to release my grip on her arms or to take my hand off her mouth. When I had turned her over, she lay motionless on the ground, not even kicking her feet anymore.

"This'll fix her," Les said, coming back with his hands and arms full of yellow muck. "She's had it coming to her for a long time. Maybe it'll stop her from being a tattletale tit."

He dropped the mass on her back and ran back for some more.

"Rub that in while I'm getting another load, Jack," he said. "That's what she needs to make her stop throwing dead limbs into the creek. She won't tell any more tales about us either."

I reached over and with one hand smeared the muck up and down Jenny's back, on her legs, and over her arms and shoulders. I tried not to get any of it in her hair, because I knew how hard it was to try to wash it out with yellow creek water.

"Turn her over," Les said, dropping down beside us with a new load of muck. "We're just getting started on her."

I turned Jenny over again, and she did not even try to get loose from me. Les had begun to spread the muck over her, rubbing it into her skin. He took a handful and smeared it over her legs and thighs and stomach. Then he took another handful and rubbed it over her shoulders and breasts. Jenny still did not attempt to move, though she squirmed a little when Les rubbed the most tender parts of her body with the mass of rotted leaves and mud. Most of the time she lay as still as if she had been sound asleep.

"That's funny," I said.

"What's funny?" Les asked, looking up.

"She's not even trying to get loose now."

"That's because she's foxy," Les said. "She's just waiting for a good chance to break away. Here, let me hold her a while."

Les took my place and I picked up a handful of muck and began spreading it over her. The muck was not sticky any longer, and when I smeared it on her, it felt slick and smooth. When my hands moved over her, I could feel that her body was much softer than mine, and that parts of her were very soft. When I smeared the slick mud over her breasts, it felt so smooth and soft that I was afraid to touch her there again. I glanced at her face, and I saw her looking at me. From the way she looked at me, I could not help thinking that she was not angry with us for treating her like that. I even thought that perhaps if Les had not been there she would have let me mud-cake her as long as I wished to.

"What are you doing, Jack?" Les said. "That's a funny way to spread muck on her."

"We've got enough on her, Les. Let's not put any more on her. Let's let her go home now. She's had enough."

"What's the matter with you?" Les said, scowling. "We're not half finished with her yet. We've got to put another coat of muck on her."

Jenny looked up when Les said that, and her eyes opened wider. She did not have to speak to tell me what she wished to say.

"That's enough, Les," I said. "She's a girl. That's enough for a girl."

170

I don't know, but somehow I believed that Les felt the same way I did, only he did not want to admit it. Now that we had stripped her and had smeared her all over with the muck, neither of us could forget that Jenny was a girl. We had treated her as though she were a boy but still she remained a girl.

"If we let you up now, will you promise not to yell?" Les asked her.

Jenny nodded her head, and Les dropped his hand from her mouth.

We both expected to hear her say what she was going to do, and what she was going to tell, because of the way we had treated her; but the moment she was freed she sat up quickly and tried to cover herself with her arms, without once speaking.

As soon as we saw that she was not going to call for Old Howes, Les and I ran to the creek and dived head-on into it. We squatted down until only our heads were showing above the water and began scrubbing the muck off us. Jenny looked at us, covering herself as much as she could.

She still had not said anything to us.

"Let's get dressed and run for home," Les said. "Pa would tear me up into little pieces if he caught me down here now, with her like that."

Jenny covered her eyes while we dashed out of the water and grabbed our clothes. We ran behind the bushes to dress. While we were standing there, we could hear Jenny splashing in the creek, scrubbing the muck from her.

Les had only his shirt and pants to put on, and he was ready to go before I could even straighten out my union suit. He buckled his pants and started backing off with his shirttail hanging out while he tried to find the right buttons for the buttonholes. I had been in such a hurry to jump into the creek when we first came that I had tangled my union suit, and when I would get the arms straight, the legs would be wrong side out. Les kept backing farther and farther away from me.

"What's the matter?" he said. "Why don't you hurry?"

"I can't get this union suit untangled."

"That's what you get for wearing underclothes in summer."

"I can't help it," I said, "and you know it."

"Well, it's not my fault, is it?"

"Aren't you going to wait for me?"

"I can't, Jack," he said, backing away faster. He suddenly turned around and began running. "I've got to go home."

"I thought you said you weren't scared of Old Howes, or of anybody else!" I yelled after him, but if he heard me, he pretended not to understand what I had said.

After Les had gone, I took my time. There was no need to hurry, because I was certain that no matter what time I got home, Jenny would tell Old Howes what we had done to her, and he would come and tell my folks all about it. I wished to have plenty of time to think of what I was going to say when I had to face everyone and tell the truth.

Jenny had left the creek by the time I was ready to button my shirt, and she had only to slip her underclothes over her head and to put on her dress to be ready to go home. She came through the bushes while I was still fumbling with my shirt buttons.

"What's the matter, Jack?" she asked, smiling just a little. "Why didn't you run off with Leslie?"

"I couldn't get dressed any quicker," I said.

I was about to tell her how my union suit was so tangled that I had had to spend most of the time struggling with that, but I thought better of saying it.

She came several steps closer, and I started to run from her.

"Where are you going?" she said. "What are you running for?"

I stopped, turned around, and looked at Jenny. Now that she was dressed, she looked the same as she had always looked. She was the same in appearance, but somehow I knew that she was not the same, after what had happened beside the creek. I could not forget the sensation I had felt when my hands, slick with mud, had touched the softness of her body. As I looked at her, I believed I felt it again, because I knew that without the dress and the underclothes she would always remain the same as she was when I had first touched her.

"Why don't you wait for me, Jack?" she said.

I wanted to run away from her, and I wanted to run to her. I stood still while she came closer.

"But you're going to tell, aren't you? Aren't you going to tell what we did to you?"

She had come to where I stood, and I turned and walked beside her, several feet away. We went through the bushes and out through the woods to the road. There was no one in sight, and we walked together until we reached her house.

Just before we got to the gate I felt my hand touch hers. I don't know, but somehow, whether it was true or not, I believed she had taken my hand and held it in hers for a moment. When I suddenly looked to see, because I wanted to know if she really had taken my hand and squeezed it, she turned the other way and went through the gate.

I waited in the middle of the road until she walked up the front steps and crossed the porch. She stopped there a moment and brushed her dress with her hands, as if she wanted to be sure that there was no muck clinging to it. When she opened the door and went inside, I was not certain whether she had glanced at me over her shoulder, or whether I merely imagined she had. Anyway, I believed she had, because I felt her looking at me, just as I was sure that she had held my hand for a moment.

"Jenny won't tell," I said, running up the road toward home. "Jenny won't tell," I kept saying over and over again all the way there.

INDEX